BOOKS BATTLES & BEES

A Readers' Competition Resource for Intermediate Grades

Sybilla Avery Cook
Cheryl A. Page

American Library Association
Chicago and London 1994

Cover design by Raymond A. Jones Graphics

Text design and composition by Charles Bozett in Galliard using QuarkXPress

Printed on 50-pound Glatfelter, a pH-neutral stock, and bound in 10-point C1S
cover stock by McNaughton & Gunn Lithographers, Inc.

The paper used in this publication meets the minimum requirements of American
National Standard for Information Sciences—Permanence of Paper for Printed
Library Materials, ANSI Z39.48-1984. ∞

The figure of the Knight that appears in chapter 4 is adapted from the Print Shop®
Graphics Library. © 1988, 1993 Brøderbund Software, Inc.
All Rights Reserved. Used by permission

Library of Congress Cataloging-in-Publication Data
Cook, Sybilla Avery, 1930–
    Books, battles, and bees : a readers' competition resource for
  intermediate grades / Sybilla Avery Cook & Cheryl A. Page.
      p.   cm.
    Includes bibliographical references (p.).
    ISBN 0-8389-0626-5 (alk. paper)
    1. Children's libraries—Activity programs—United States.
  2. Elementary school libraries—Activity programs—United States.
  3. Book contests. 4. Children's literature—Study and teaching
  (Elementary)—United States. I. Page, Cheryl A. II. Title.
  Z718.2.U6C66 1993
  027.8'223'0973—dc20   93-29756

Printed in the United States of America.

98 97 96 95 94   5 4 3 2 1

To A.J.
for all her love and dedication,
and to T.P., J.P., and K.P.
for their gift of time;

and in memory of Marjorie Williams,
former coordinator of the
Instructional Materials Centers
District 62, Des Plaines, Illinois

Contents

Figures   vii

Preface   ix

PART 1   The Book Quiz Programs   1

     CHAPTER 1   From Then to Now   3

         From Radio to Reality   4
         Creating the Program   5

     CHAPTER 2   Beginnings   7

         Choosing the Format   7
         Who Will Take Part?   9
         Choosing the Books   10

     CHAPTER 3   Questions   13

         Writing the Questions   14
         Scoring   16
         Thinking Skills   18

     CHAPTER 4   The Battles   22

         Preliminaries   22
         When and Where   24
         Publicity   26
         Supplementary Materials   26
         Rules   30
         Tournaments and Play-offs   32

CHAPTER 5   A Timeline for Planning   39

PART 2   The Questions   43

Appendices   137

Author List   137
Easier Books   145
More Advanced Books   147
Animals   149
Historical Settings   151
Classics: Old and New   153
Humor   154
Mystery and Adventure   156
Fantasy and Magic   157
Newbery Award and Honor Books   159
Regional Award
Pacific Northwest Library Association
Young Reader's Choice Books   162

Bibliography   165

Figures

3.1   Blank Score Sheet   17

4.1   Book Identification   23

4.2   Reminder Schedule for Teachers   25

4.3   Classroom Reminder Notice   26

4.4   Battle Notice for Bulletin Board   27

4.5   Bookmarks   28

4.6   Team Badges and Tags   29

4.7   Invitations   31

4.8   Scores and Team Rankings   33

4.9   16 Teams Ranked in Order of Scores   34

4.10   10 Teams Ranked in Order of Scores   34

4.11   16 Teams, Paired Off for Brackets   35

4.12   10 Teams, Paired Off for Brackets   35

4.13   A 16-Team Tournament Play-off   36

4.14   A 10-Team Tournament Play-off   37

5.1   Newsletter Article   41

Preface

Quiz programs have always been popular, whether the old game of "animal, vegetable or mineral," or the newer TV game shows such as "Jeopardy!" and "Wheel of Fortune." They're also a form of entertainment often used as motivation for learning. Spelling bees, for example, have traditionally been used for entertainment, motivation and reinforcement.

Quiz games and programs based on knowledge of books are similar adaptations. They can range from a simple impromptu car game based on twenty questions—"I'm thinking of a book." "Is it about an animal?"—to a very formal structure such as "Battle of the Books." The milieu can range from the intimacy of the family dinner table to the public exposure of a television show.

Book quiz programs are a great method for developing school or public library partnerships. Our book is targeted to teachers and librarians who work with children in a library setting. Since we are both school library media specialists, our book has a definite school slant. However, it can certainly be used by those who work in public libraries.

We have chosen to target intermediate and upper-grade children, which we define as those in grades 3-8. At these ages they are enthusiastic about using their reading skills, are willing to try many types of books, and enjoy competitive activities. We have emphasized the "Battle of the Books" because this is a well-known program that has been going on for over fifty years, and one that can be easily adapted to fit individual needs.

"Battle of the Books" has a long history. Our personal involvement came from Norma L. Rogers and Robin M. Caton, two librarians at the Urbana Free Library in Urbana, Illinois. This library sponsored the play-offs for the local school district. The enthusiasm of the public and school librarians in Urbana led to the adoption of the "Battle of the Books" program by other Illinois districts, including the Des Plaines School District where Sybilla Cook was once employed.

Fran Corcoran and Bridget Doerner, library media specialists in Des Plaines, wrote Mrs. Cook about how much their students were enjoying the program. They were willing to share the questions that had been compiled by the entire Des Plaines media staff, which also included Pat Daniels, Barb Dochterman, Jan Doherty, Roslyn Goodman, Marian Hill, and Ruth Rico.

With this list, Mrs. Cook was able to begin this project at the Glide Elementary School in Glide, Oregon. Patricia Feehan, then the children's consultant at the Oregon State Library, had previously learned of the "Battle of the Books" when located in Michigan, and shared many of her ideas for the program. Martin Hilgers, Stan Johns, Patricia Fugate, and Patricia Boyd gave enthusiastic support.

Cheryl Page heard about the successful Glide program, and became interested in adopting the idea to the Winston-Dillard school district. She borrowed Mrs. Cook's question bank, and added her own ideas and questions to the collection.

Since we both found that question writing was the most intimidating and time-consuming aspect of the program, we decided to share the questions we had written with others. We have included five questions each for 250 different books that are commonly read in the intermediate grades. The books have been selected from various standard lists such as *Children's Catalog* and the *Elementary School Library Collection,* or are those we have found to be favorites among our students and teachers. In addition to many of the Newbery Award winners and honor books, we have included most of the books that have received the Young Reader's Choice Award from the Pacific Northwest Library Association. Penny Clark from Elkton Grade School, Judy Kulluson from Eastwood School, and Aletha Cox and Charles Kamilos of the Douglas County Library System also suggested some favorite titles to include.

The books we've used with the questions we've written for them are listed by title in one alphabetical list. This should make it easy for you to find everything on any particular book you wish to use. The appendices contain an alphabetical list of authors, a list of books we consider to be at an easier level of understanding, and a list of those we consider more advanced. There are also several lists categorized by subject.

We owe great thanks to all the people mentioned above. Jim McClellan, Bonnie Smothers, Susan DeFelice, and Steve Mesner also contributed their expertise. We couldn't have begun our programs without everyone's help and encouragement. This seems to be typical of the way most of these programs begin. Librarians and school library media specialists have always shared their successful ideas through various informal and formal networks of newsletters, workshops, and library conferences. Collaboration and cooperation are what make all these programs work, and what has helped them spread across the country.

We hope that our book will inspire more librarians and media specialists to begin this project in their own locales, and will make it easier for them to get started. Our desire is to add another link to the long chain of librarians who continually try to keep children connected with the many good books that make up our literary heritage.

1

The
Book Quiz Programs

1

From Then to Now

How would you like to run a program in your library media center that: Turns many students on to reading? Involves their teachers? Is truly integrated with the language, literature, and reading programs? Expands the choice of books that teachers read aloud to their students? Increases book circulation and library usage? Brings parents in to see what their kids are doing? Creates positive publicity?

If all this sounds interesting, try various book contests such as "Battle of the Books." These do all of the above. They complement language arts programs by providing motivation for children to read an assortment of well-chosen fiction and non-fiction books. They are also self-perpetuating annual events. As soon as our students return in September they start asking when the book battles will begin.

Book contests are great incentives for leisure reading. They are also a great method for selling books to teachers and parents as well as students, and they bring attention to many worthwhile books that are not necessarily the most popular or well known. Reading the same books creates a common denominator of experience among students. Books can be chosen to reflect any subject or theme such as award winners, historical fiction, or family life; or they can be an eclectic mixture chosen to provide a wide range of reading experience.

Using a well-known program such as "Battle of the Books" gives reading high visibility, and is an excellent public relations tool for the school library media center. Administration, staff, and community members can become actively involved in this venture, which then also becomes an ideal subject for newspaper or television school features.

These programs take some extra planning time before launching, as does any successful program. However, our book is designed to give you the information you need to help you get the program started with the least amount of effort. You will find that while it takes only a minimum amount of work to keep it going after the first year, the momentum and enthusiasm keep increasing. At last year's graduation, the high school salutatorian summed up the school events that her class remembered as important. Our book quiz program was cited as one of those experiences remembered from elementary school days—a real validation of the program!

Book quizzes can be varied. Some school library media specialists use computerized quiz programs produced by outside companies. In these programs students work alone, competing against themselves as they answer computer-generated questions on the books they have read. Other programs such as battles, bees, bowls, and circles are group oriented, and take place with live audiences. These competitive formats appeal to children in the upper grades. They enjoy playing against others of similar age or ability. Those who excel in reading have a chance to gain the same type of recognition accorded to those who excel in athletics.

From Radio to Reality

The "Battle of the Books" program has been gaining in popularity throughout the United States. This is a team competition with questions about specific books read by all the participants. It began in the 1930s as a project in the Chicago school system. Ruth Harshaw was the educational consultant for the Carson, Pirie Scott department store, and Dilla MacBean was the director of school libraries in the Chicago public schools. The women got together "over teacups" and discovered they both shared a love of children and reading, as well as a belief that "every experience that a child has, everything he thinks, may be enriched with books."[1] Together, they developed a radio quiz show for the Chicago Board of Education, using teams of students from two different Chicago schools each week.[2] The popular show was followed up by the publication of two books of questions for use by other teachers and librarians. Ruth Harshaw and Dilla MacBean wrote *What Book Is That?* in 1948.[3] This book included dramatic sketches based on children's books, in addition to the suggested questions. Ruth Harshaw's second book, *In What Book?*, was completed in 1970 after her death by her grand-daughter Hope Harshaw Evans.[4] Although both these books are out-of-print, they are worth reading for the sense of caring projected throughout.

This original "Battle of Books" program was later adapted for use in other school districts. Joanne Kelly, a school library media specialist at the Thomas Paine School in Urbana, Illinois, had been a child participant in the Chicago radio program. Looking for a way to promote reading, she reconstructed it from memory and began it in her own school.[5] The battles in the individual Urbana schools were followed by tournament play-offs at the public library, complete with prizes donated by local businesses. She later wrote about the program in *School Library Journal*.[6] From this beginning, the project spread across the country.

Most library media specialists who decide to adopt this type of project revise it to fit the needs of their particular school or setting. There are probably almost as many adaptations of "Battle of the Books" as there are school districts. *School Librarian's Workshop*, a journal of practical ideas by and for school library media specialists, has published several articles on various ways librarians adapt it to different age groups and school situations.

Alaska is an outstanding example of adapting to suit local circumstances. Roslyn Goodman and other school librarians have pioneered an audio conference program using LEARN ALASKA, the state's telecommunication system. This enables students in even the most isolated schools to compete with others who are geographically far away.[7] Shades of Ruth Harshaw's radio show!

Creating the Program

Any organized book program demands time and attention. There are many things to consider in advance before the program begins. What type of program format will best suit your circumstances? Will it take place within one classroom, one grade, or be school-wide? Will it be formally structured or fairly free, evolving to fit the time available? If it is school-wide, with a formal structure, when and where will it take place? Will there be any involvement from other schools or other libraries within the community?

Who are the students who will take part? What criteria will be used to select them? Will they be chosen by teachers? Or can any interested student take part?

What books will you expect students to read for this program? What reading level? How many books? How will the books be chosen?

What kinds of questions will you use? How many? Who will develop the questions? Students, teachers, library personnel, or all of these?

You may wish to begin with just one class, using a simple program like the book bee, and then move to a more formal program. Or you may wish to begin with a full-fledged program such as "Battle of the Books." This book attempts to give you enough background so that you can design a program that fits your particular needs. We will cover different kinds of programs, the choice of students, the choice of books, and how to write the questions. We have also included questions on many books that are read in the elementary and middle school grades.

NOTES

1. Ruth Harshaw and Dilla MacBean, *What Book Is That? Fun with Books at Home, at School* (New York: Macmillan, 1948), p. 8.

2. Ruth Harshaw and Hope Harshaw Evans, *In What Book?* (New York: Macmillan, 1970), p. ix.

3. Harshaw and MacBean, *What Book Is That?*

4. Harshaw and Evans, *In What Book?*

5. Joanne Kelly, *Battle of Books: K-8* (Littleton, Colorado: Teacher Ideas Press, a division of Libraries Unlimited, 1990) p. xii.

6. Joanne Kelly, "'Battle of Books' Urbana Style," *School Library Journal* (October 1982): 105-8.

7. Alaska Association of School Librarians, "Battle of the Books Handbook," 1985, 1990-91.

2

Beginnings

Y ou will need to do a lot of advance planning so that the program will run smoothly. Begin slowly, on a small scale, and let the program expand and adapt to meet individual needs. Once established, it will keep running on its own momentum.

Enthusiasm is always the key in beginning successful projects. Start with a few eager teachers in one class or grade. Other students and grades can be added as the project grows and progresses.

Book bees, bowls, or battles can take place at any level or grade in a school, from primary to high school. We begin our program in grade 4, since this is the age when students are open to trying different types of books, and when most can enjoy a competition without being overwhelmed by the prospect of losing.

Choosing the Format

Quiz contests can take many forms, depending on the needs of the school. Teachers often use baseball, basketball, and football as models for motivational games. Students who answer questions correctly may advance paper footballs on a chalkboard field, shoot sponge basketballs into a net, or move around the room from chairs representing bases.

Book bees or book circles are also often used to motivate students. The book bee is arranged like the standard spelling bee, with children divided into two teams which stand on the opposite sides of the room. Questions are asked of one child. If the question is answered correctly, it goes to another member of the same team. If the question is missed, the child who misses it sits down, and the next one is asked of the other team. (Some schools give each student a chance to answer two questions before they have to sit down.) The questions continue until only one child remains standing. Joanne Kelly creates teams within a classroom situation by drawing an imaginary line across the room. Children sitting on one side of the line are on one team.[1]

The circle format has all participants sitting in a circle around the classroom. The teacher gives the question to the first student. If that child cannot answer, the next child has a chance to try, and so on around the circle until the question is answered. A new question is then asked of another student. This is a bit less threatening than the bee, because everyone remains in the circle, no matter how many questions are missed. One advantage of the bee and circle formats is that everyone in a class is involved, rather than a chosen few.

A disadvantage of the bee and circle formats is that students know when they will be expected to answer, and may not pay attention until near their turn. Another disadvantage was pointed out to me by Susan, a student who participated in a circle format. She was always seated next to Heather, an avid reader. As the questions went around the circle, they went first to Heather who usually was able to answer. Susan, then, received a brand new question and had little time to think about the answer.

One way of solving these problems is to have the student who answers the question choose a student to begin the next round of questioning. If the questions usually travel in a clockwise direction, they can be switched to travel counter-clockwise occasionally. In Mesa, Arizona, they have the students draw lots for their seating positions.[2] You can also shuffle students at a given signal, or have the students change seats every so often.

The bowl or battle format requires teams. Primary teachers usually make the team assignments, because they know the ability levels and also know which children work well together. Children at the intermediate level or above usually choose their own teammates. They may be from the same classroom or grade, but this is not necessary. The varied educational experiences of multigrade and other heterogeneous teams can give them a real advantage.

Three to five members make up a team in most schools. We have always preferred four-member teams, with a rule that no substitutes are allowed. If someone is absent, the team still plays even though one member is not present. Why? Because a few years ago we discovered that some teams were pressuring their weaker members not to come to school on a battle day. It turned out that there was a really good reader in the sixth grade who they wanted to have as a substitute! Some schools get around this problem by keeping a list of alternates from which the school library media specialist chooses a substitute.

We also found it to be a good idea not to allow any changes in the makeup of a team after it's formed. Otherwise the worst enemy-best friend syndrome leads to constant chaotic change. Friendships in the upper grades are often extremely volatile!

Teams may choose a name for themselves. Some like to make their own buttons to wear during battles. T-shirts can also be created with names or logos by using various computer graphic programs.[3]

Once the teams are formed and named, they sign up for battles. There are several ways in which this can be accomplished. We like to begin by matching up teams of similar ability levels. In some schools teams put their name on a slip which is placed in a box. A random drawing determines which teams play on a given time and date. In still others, a chart of battle times is posted in the hall or media center, and students themselves sign up for any open slots.

Who Will Take Part?

After you decide on the format you want to use, the next decision to make is about the grades that you want to involve, and how the participants will be chosen. Book quizzes such as bees and battles are often promoted as something just for gifted children. However, we feel this project is not only for the talented and gifted, but also for every student. As Joanne Kelly emphasizes, "You don't have to be wonderful, just willing."[4] Reading books is something that every child can do, and a competition often creates both interest and enthusiasm that can carry students beyond their identified reading levels. It turns a solitary activity into a cooperative one. The knowledge of books and authors becomes important to many students, and this provides additional motivation for reading.

We used to be surprised when we found non-readers chosen for a team. This was obviously due to friendship, rather than ability. However, we discovered that though these children weren't good participants initially, they usually began to read in order to help their team win.

Make sure it's a very positive experience for everyone involved. Students should value their own effort, achievement and knowledge. Play down the competitive factor in the lower grades. Use the circle format where every child has a chance, or some simple library book game such as the "Jeopardy!" adaptation developed by Rosemary Trotier.[5] Competition is important and fun for students in the upper grades, but still needs to be kept fairly low key so as to prevent a high anxiety level. Encourage children to do their personal best and contribute to the team performance, rather than concentrating solely on the scores.

You'll find that these quiz contests promote a great deal of social interaction and cooperative learning among students, giving them the opportunity to work together in a team situation. It's really interesting to see how children organize their preparation. Some read only the books on the list that interest them, and don't worry about anything else. Other groups become very organized, and assign each team member a certain number of titles. Some children spend their noon hours exchanging comments about the books, and then quizzing each other.

Choosing the Books

The choice of books is vital. You want a good variety of *readable* books including prizewinners, new books, and traditional modern classics. Have a variety of types, so that students will have a chance to try reading different genres (our appendices include several different categories of the listed books). Consider length, degree of difficulty, and theme. Solicit suggestions for the books from teachers and students. We always include some of the teachers' favorite "readalouds," because children are familiar with them.

Most state library associations annually honor outstanding children's books, and these titles make excellent choices. School districts often have recommended or required reading lists. California has a list of recommended books for all their school libraries, and other states have similar lists as well.[6]

Students need to feel successful, so start with the easier and more familiar books. Harder ones can be added later. Although you want books that have some depth to them, they do not have to be difficult books. For example, *Sarah Plain and Tall* and *Winnie the Pooh* are short and easy to read, but both provide a wealth of ideas to think and talk about.[7]

Most publisher's series books do not make very good subjects for questions. These books are usually written to a formula, with the same main characters and patterns of events. For example, Donald J. Sobol's Encyclopedia Brown books have different incidents in them, but almost any episode could fit in any of the books. Beverly Cleary's Ramona books are an exception to this rule because Ramona grows and changes from year to year, with different teachers and grades. Even so, only one of these books should be used in any given year.

At inventory time note the books that are currently being overlooked by students and teachers, and stick a marker on the shelflist cards of books that shouldn't be forgotten. Add some of these to next year's list. Since teachers often use these book lists to choose new "readalouds" for their classroom, this is a way of bringing these "oldies but goodies" to everyone's attention.

The number of books on the list varies from school to school, depending on the type of competition being used, the children who participate, and the library's collection of books. Some schools use as few as ten at a time, while others may use up to one hundred. Alaska's official book list has fifteen books for each of their participating grade levels: K-2, 3-4, 5-6, 7-8, and high school.[8] The Des Plaines School District begins with ten books in the first November round, then adds another ten books in January, another ten in February, and still another ten in March.[9]

After the media specialist prepares a book list, some teachers will expand their own knowledge of books and read aloud some of the suggested books. Parents frequently request a copy of the book list for themselves. Sometimes the discovery of an overlooked author or title will lead to the reading of other books which are not listed. Parents often remember and remark upon these programs as really turning their children on to reading. Once children have the ability to read on their own, the book quiz concept can be used to encourage them to continue.

Change the list of books from one year to the next. Many of the same children participate every time, and you do want to keep them reading. If there are one hundred books on a list, then twenty to twenty-five should be changed annually. A smaller book list may need to be totally revised. Be sure to keep track of the titles used each year. We found that a computerized database such as *Appleworks* helps keep track of book titles and the years in which they appear on the list

NOTES

1. Joanne Kelly, *Battle of Books: K-8* (Littleton, Colorado: Teacher Ideas Press, a division of Libraries Unlimited, 1990), p. 3.

2. "The Battles Continue," *School Librarian's Workshop* (November 1986): 8.

3. Apple Computer's *MacPaint* and Broderbund's *Print Shop* are two programs with the ability to reverse the graphics. Most computer supply companies should have transfer ribbons to fit your printer. They can also be ordered from BriteLine, a division of Pixellite, Inc., 3065 Research Drive, Richmond, CA 94806.

4. Joanne Kelly, "'The Battle of Books'—the Urbana Way," *School Librarian's Workshop* (April 1986): 3.

5. Rosemary Trotier, "Follow This Game Plan," *School Library Journal* (February 1989): 34.

6. Lists of these usually can be obtained from your state library association. Charlotte Huck's book, *Children's Literature in the Elementary School,* 4th ed. (New York: Holt, 1987), gives the addresses of most award committees in appendix A, pp. 733-38. Dolores Blyth Jones lists winners in *Children's Literature Awards and Winners: A Directory of Prizes, Authors and Illustrators,* 2nd ed. (Detroit: Neal-Schuman and Gale Research, 1988). Another list of present and past winners can be found in *Children's Books: Awards and Prizes,* which may be obtained from the Children's Book Council, 67 Irving Place, New York, NY 10003.

7. Patricia MacLachlan, *Sarah Plain and Tall* (New York: Harper, 1984); A. A. Milne, *Winnie the Pooh* (New York: Dutton, 1926).

8. Alaska Association of School Librarians, "Battle of the Books Handbook," 1985, 1990-91.

9. District No. 62, "Presenting Battle of the Books" (Des Plaines, Illinois, [1980]).

3

Questions

Our books and questions are aimed at students in grades 4-6. Most of the books we have chosen are generally read in the intermediate and upper grades. The levels of reading and comprehension range from third grade through junior high school. Your collection should have enough of these titles to cover your first year or two of battles.

Since we feel that writing questions is time-consuming, we have given five questions for each of the 262 books on our list. Five questions will be enough to launch the project; you will probably need to add some more of your own as the battles continue.

Several other books containing usable questions have already been published. Besides the books by Harshaw and Evans, a recent book by Greeson and Taha offers questions on computer disks as well as in print form.[1] Joanne Kelly's book, *Battle of Books: K-8,* also includes a disk version.[2]

For an additional fee, The Electronic Bookshelf book company will include a set of five questions with some of the books you purchase from them.[3] Other books and articles that can expand your stock of questions are listed in the bibliography. Another very helpful idea is the cooperation between public library and school in the creation of battle questions, as is done in Des Plaines.[4] Once you have established an original core of books and questions, you'll find it is fairly easy to keep up with year to year additions. The questions you create yourself, aimed at your own particular students, will be the ones you will finally prefer using. It's fun to go through the books selecting the parts that seem most vivid to you, while also thinking of individual children who will be wrestling with the questions you are writing.

Most of the questions we have used over the years are knowledge and comprehension questions, relying on memory. These are simple in structure, test a student's general knowledge of the book, and can be answered by almost anyone who has read the book. Even though these are simple, there are several points to follow in their creation.

Writing the Questions

After choosing the books that you're going to use, start rereading them with paper and pencil in hand. Make a card for each question. Index cards are easy to handle, or the backs of old catalog cards can be recycled for this. Make sure you write the name of the author and the title of the book on each card—you may find yourself forgetting these under pressure! Because you will not want the questions to be easily read by anyone other than the quizmaster, use small handwriting. If you put the questions on a computer disk, make sure you use the smallest font size available when you print them out. Some children are amazingly adept in reading from a distance!

Most of the questions we have included in this book are those we have developed and used for many years. These will help you to begin your program. As you continue to work with the program, you will find yourself modifying our questions and creating your own to suit your own style and your own students.

Harshaw's original questions are quite diverse, requiring many comparisons, and demanding a knowledge of quotations, authors, and a wide variety of literature. The answers can be varied. In the more recent format that we have used, the questions are phrased so that the answer is always the book title. Children know what to expect, and the time frame for the battles stays the same.

Even with a standard format, you can make the questions interesting. Use colorful and memorable details. Don't use questions that give away the book's ending. You'll find that your questions often sell a particular book to members of the audience—another side benefit of the program.

With a large list of books, you will need a minimum of four or five questions for each book. This will give you some to use during regular battles, plus one or two harder ones to keep in reserve for playoffs. If you have a small list, you will need to have more questions. You can reuse questions, but if the same one is used too often, some children will begin to memorize the answers.

Try to vary the content of the questions you write. Avoid tricky questions, because you want this to be an enjoyable project, not a test. You may wish to include a few "giveaway" questions in your first few battles. These give students confidence. Surprisingly, sometimes questions which seem to be too easy actually turn out to stump some kids.

Questions can be devised on setting, character, plot or theme. They can range from a very broad topic in the book to a very specific question on an event. Quotations from the book also make good questions.

The questions should be fairly short. If they are too wordy, kids may forget the beginning of the question by the time you get to the end. Although the questions need to be brief, sometimes brevity or paraphrasing can cause a problem by not properly representing the particular book. *Reread all questions before using them.*

The vocabulary used in the question should reflect the vocabulary used in the book. As you use and reuse the questions, you'll find that you naturally rephrase them to fit your own speaking patterns.

Questions need to be very specific and fit only one book on the list. "In what book does a four-year-old girl ride her trike across the game being played by her sister?" is much more specific to Ramona Quimby than "In what book is a little girl considered a pest by her older sister?"[5]

It's difficult to write questions that are specific to a particular book of non-fiction, such as biographies. For example, there are many biographies of Daniel Boone, and it can be hard to make sure that your questions pertain to incidents solely within the award winner by Daugherty.[6] This can also be true of fiction adaptations of well-known incidents. Our list includes two versions of the journey of the Sager children on the Oregon Trail, for example: *On to Oregon* by Morrow and *The Stout-Hearted Seven* by Frazier.[7] Each book includes different incidents, but we still only use one of these books in a particular year.

Folklore can be tricky for the same reason. Our questions on King Arthur, for example, can apply to several versions. If you use these, make sure you have a question or two that can be answered only from the version you have decided to use. You can always make a question apply to your own particular title by beginning the question with "In which book on our list . . ." instead of "In what book . . .."

Sometimes you may need to use a character's name in order to make the question apply to a particular book. It's usually best, however, to avoid using a character's name if it is part of the title of the book. You can use such generic terms such as "heroine," "boy," or "main character." Even if the character's name isn't part of the title, it often gives a very strong hint. However, use it when you feel the need to make a question easier.

Watch out for questions that can be answered by reading the brief annotations on catalog cards or a book jacket. Do make sure that the question is based on the original book, rather than a different version. Sometimes films and videos have different incidents and characters.

Don't use trivia, items which really don't matter to the story. For example, clothing is generally unimportant. On the other hand, sometimes an article of clothing is quite distinctive to a character and can make a good question: Pippi Longstocking's mismatched stockings, for example, or Sam Gribley's rabbit skin underwear.[8]

The question, "What book is about a little girl who lives in Wisconsin?" is poor because it can have many answers: Laura Ingalls Wilder's or Anne Pellowski's books or *Caddie Woodlawn*. However, you may wish to have students do some comparative thinking. If you want to stress the similarities between books, change the above question to "Name at least one book in which a little girl was a pioneer in Wisconsin"; or "Name at least one book in which a pioneer girl sided with the Indians."[9]

Scoring

How many points will students receive for answering the questions correctly? You might be very simple and give one point for each correct title, and another for each correct author. Perhaps someone could get a bonus point, for a total of three points if both parts of the question are answered. Most schools give five points for a correct title, and three points for the correct rendition of the author's name.

Create score sheets to be used for the battles (figure 3.1), with room for twenty questions. This makes it easy to check the answers

BATTLE OF

_____

Date _____

Team #1 Names: _____	Team #2 Names: _____
	_____
	_____
	_____

Title	Author		Title	Author	Audience
1. _____	_____		_____	_____	_____
2. _____	_____		_____	_____	_____
3. _____	_____		_____	_____	_____
4. _____	_____		_____	_____	_____
5. _____	_____		_____	_____	_____
6. _____	_____		_____	_____	_____
7. _____	_____		_____	_____	_____
8. _____	_____		_____	_____	_____
9. _____	_____		_____	_____	_____
10. _____	_____		_____	_____	_____
11. _____	_____		_____	_____	_____
12. _____	_____		_____	_____	_____
13. _____	_____		_____	_____	_____
14. _____	_____		_____	_____	_____
15. _____	_____		_____	_____	_____
16. _____	_____		_____	_____	_____
17. _____	_____		_____	_____	_____
18. _____	_____		_____	_____	_____
19. _____	_____		_____	_____	_____
20. _____	_____		_____	_____	_____

Figure 3.1 Blank Score Sheet

in the appropriate column as each team takes their turn. If the question is not answered, the corresponding column is left blank. It's then very simple to tally the total points at the end.

You also need to decide how much time you will give children to respond. Usually thirty seconds is enough time for intermediate students to come up with the answer. If a team misses the question, the question goes to the other team, but they only have five seconds to come up with the answer. That is because they have already heard this question, and have had time to consider their response.

Thinking Skills

Some schools or teachers feel that the battles should contain more than knowledge and comprehension questions. They feel this type of project should demand more advanced levels of thinking and understanding. The article on "Greater Dimensions for the Battle of the Books" in *School Librarian's Workshop* addresses this topic, referring to the six cognitive levels of knowledge, comprehension, application, synthesis, analysis, and evaluation in Bloom's taxonomy.[10]

Certainly comparison and analysis questions can be used within a battle. Questions can be created about a common theme, such as survival, a historical period, or particular characters. Those on pioneer Wisconsin, cited above, are one example. Another example might be "Name at least one book in which insects are among the main characters."[11]

An occasional contest could also be created to stress these skills. For example, you could ask "Name at least one way in which *The True Confessions of Charlotte Doyle* is like *The Slave Dancer*."[12] Possible answers might refer to the sailing ship setting, the fact that both books take place in the 1800s, or that both books have captains at odds with their crews. A correct answer would be worth five points, and knowledge of the author would be two points. You could allow the other team to add another item, or to challenge an answer they feel is wrong.

Thinking skills can also be developed through the use of "why" questions. Ruth Harshaw's original book contains many questions of this type.[13] These can also focus attention on the idea of consequences—that specific actions cause specific events. For example: "Why did Billy eat an ice-cream cake with worms?" or "Why were

Dicey and her brothers and sisters walking to Aunt Cilla's instead of going by bus?" One book that lends itself really well to this type of approach is Avi's 1991 Newbery Honor Book, *Nothing But the Truth* (Orchard 1991), which shows just how a minor action can escalate into a crisis. This book is most appropriate for the junior high or middle school student.

If you use this sort of question, give five points for the answer, with three points for the title and two points for the author. You will also need to allow more time for the contest, since the questions will take longer to answer. Classroom teachers can follow up by having students develop possible alternate outcomes.

Another method of encouraging other levels of thinking is to involve students in reading discussion groups such as *Junior Great Books*.[14] Students learn to use the specific concepts in the book itself as a basis for discussion, rather than relying on their own knowledge or ideas. They learn to group and categorize books in terms of concept and theme.

Many teachers and librarians make up supplementary activity project cards for students. Some of these also incorporate other types of thinking skills. For example, one activity suggested in the Alaska handbook is the use of computer programs to create a crossword puzzle on individual books.[15] Other ideas here include having students design a flag, banner, or coat-of-arms for the Kingdom of Terabithia, or make a game using synonyms for titles, such as "The flowers and the jade ghost."[16] There are also some useful ideas for projects in the annual Young Reader's Choice handbooks.[17]

Letting students create their own questions, as suggested in Harshaw's first book, is another way of addressing the higher level thinking skills.[18] Students at the Robson Elementary School in Mesa, Arizona, are required to write these.[19] Usually, students enjoy writing book questions that become part of later battles. For example, some Urbana children decided to create a battle for their teachers. They wrote all the questions for this with the help of the public librarians.[20] If a teacher approves, writing questions can become part of student book reports. Analyzing questions submitted by others also involves the higher-order thinking skills.

If you decide to include student created questions, keep a "question suggestion" box available in the library. You may need to demonstrate how to create questions that only apply to a particular book. Point out that not all questions submitted will be used. You will have to edit all questions for clarity, grammar and specifics, as well as making sure the questions are based on the book rather than the film. Insist that all questions include the title and author of the book, as well as the name of the person submitting it. Make sure you give verbal credit during the battles to the originator of those questions which are used.

Identical or similar questions are often submitted by students, since the same incident or character often appeals to different readers. In this case, the first person to submit the question receives the credit.

The above suggestions may seem overwhelming, but they really are not as bad as they seem. We sketch out questions as we read, noting incidents that will make good questions. The questions can be written and revised later, so it's a good idea to note the page numbers just in case! Remember that the above rules are only meant to be helpful guidelines in question writing. Your own judgment will tell you the adaptations and changes that suit your own program.

NOTES

1. Janet Greeson and Karen Taha, *Name That Book* (Metuchen, New Jersey: Scarecrow, 1986).

2. Joanne Kelly, *Battle of Books: K-8* (Littleton, Colorado: Teacher Ideas Press, a division of Libraries Unlimited, 1990).

3. A catalog is available from The Electronic Bookshelf, Inc., 5276 South Clinton Co., 700 West, Frankfort, IN 46041-8113.

4. District No. 62, "Presenting Battle of the Books" (Des Plaines, Illinois, [1980]).

5. Beverly Cleary, *Ramona the Pest* (New York: Morrow, 1968).

6. James Daugherty, *Daniel Boone* (New York: Viking, 1939).

7. Honore Morrow, *On to Oregon* (New York: Morrow, 1954); Neta Frazier, *The Stout-Hearted Seven* (New York: Harcourt, 1973).

8. Astrid Lindgren, *Pippi Longstocking* (New York: Viking, 1950); Jean George, *My Side of the Mountain* (New York: Dutton, 1959).

9. Carol Ryrie Brink, *Caddie Woodlawn* (New York: Macmillan, 1936); Laura Ingalls Wilder, *Little House on the Prairie* (New York: Harper, 1932).

10. "Greater Dimensions for the Battle of the Books," *School Librarian's Workshop* (September 1988): 1-3.

11. George Selden, *Cricket in Times Square* (New York: Farrar, Straus, 1960) and Paul Fleishman, *Joyful Noise* (New York: HarperCollins, 1988).

12. Avi, *The True Confessions of Charlotte Doyle* (New York: Orchard Books, 1990); Paula Fox, *The Slave Dancer* (New York: Bradbury, 1973).

13. Ruth Harshaw and Dilla MacBean, *What Book Is That? Fun with Books at Home, at School* (New York: Macmillan, 1948).

14. For information, write or call The Great Books Foundation, 35 East Wacker Drive, Suite 2300, Chicago, IL 60601-2298. Phone: 800-222-5870.

15. Alaska Association of School Librarians, "Battle of the Books Handbook," 1985, 1990-91.

16. Betsy Byars, *The Blossoms and the Green Phantom* (New York: Delacorte, 1987).

17. *Handbook for the Young Reader's Choice Award Nominees.* These are issued every year. Write for information to: Beyond Basals, Inc. 586 University Drive, Pocatello, ID 83201.

18. Harshaw and MacBean, *What Book Is That?*, p. 10.

19. "The 'Battles' Continue," *School Librarian's Workshop* (November 1986): 8.

20. Joanne Kelly, "'Battle of Books' Urbana Style," *School Library Journal* (October 1982): 108.

4

The Battles

Preliminaries

Once the titles are selected, you can create the list of books to be used during the current school year. Make sure that you print enough for all interested students and teachers.

Mark the books so that participants can easily distinguish the books being used from others in the library. If you use spine labels make sure they are the type to be easily peeled off later. You can also wrap strips of construction paper around the books (see figure 4.1), so they are easily spotted when returned. Or set aside a special shelf that's used only for these books.[1]

Prepare enough questions for at least two full days of battles. This is not something that you want to do at the last minute. The number of questions needed will depend on the amount of time available. We allow about fifteen minutes for each battle. Since each team has only thirty seconds in which to answer a question, we find we need about twenty questions per battle. We also keep some spare questions on hand in case of a miscount or a last minute decision not to use a particular question. Additional questions may also be used as tie-breakers.

File prepared questions in a box by the dates of the battles in which they will be used. Group questions putting two questions of comparable difficulty or familiarity together. This keeps one team from winding up with all the easy questions, while the other team gets the difficult ones. One school posts all questions face down on a

Yarn tied around
book spine to mark
a battle book

Construction paper or
mylar book wrap strip
(taped to jacket flaps
inside cover)

Figure 4.1 Book Identification

bulletin board. The questions are numbered, and teams select the number of the question to answer. The randomness of the questions make it a more exciting competition because of the element of luck involved. Questions that are missed during one battle can be filed again for use at a later date. Place a checkmark on the back of the card each time the question is used to make sure the same questions aren't repeated too often.

When and Where

If it is at all possible, allow enough time for two or three battles to take place on a given day. Each of our twenty-question battles takes about fifteen minutes. Greeson and Taha have half-hour matches, using sixty questions per match.[2]

Battle days can be scheduled every week, every other week, or at any regular interval that seems best suited to your school schedule. Scheduling battles for the winter months works well, since school schedules seem to be freer, and students have more indoor time for reading. Some schools like to center these activities around Children's Book Week or National Library Week. Plan these days well in advance, and make sure they are on the school calendar.

Teachers should have advance notice about the times when the battles will take place. We send out both advance lists and special reminders on battle days (see figures 4.2 and 4.3). We invite teachers to bring their students in to watch as long as the teachers stay with their class (this is not teacher prep time!). The audience is expected to be quiet, and not distract the students who are battling. We involve the audience by letting them answer any questions missed by both teams. We keep score for the audience and give them ten seconds to come up with the correct answer. We occasionally have had battles when the audience actually beat the teams.

Three people are needed for each battle. An adult is needed to act as the quizmaster who reads the questions to the teams. An *accurate* scorekeeper is vital. There should also be a timer who watches the clock and signals when a team's time is up. We encourage participating students to invite their parents to attend, and these interested adults are good choices for these managerial tasks. This is a wonderful way for them to be involved.

If an audience is involved, a battle will need a fairly large room. The ideal place, of course, is within the school library media center. A grouping of chairs or a table is needed for each team, so that each team is sitting together facing the audience. The quizmaster and scorekeeper need to be able to see the teams, and the timekeeper needs to see the clock. The audience sits on the floor, so that everyone is able to see the participants. At least two of the adults present should also be able to supervise the audience.

THURSDAY, MARCH 2, 1989	12:15 PM (LUNCH RECESS)	
Chicarees	VS.	**Bobkits**
ERIN		HEATHER
TRICIA		JAKE
CARRIE		SARA
ANGELA		RAY
	12:30 PM	
Timbertops	VS.	**Pages**
BOB		MARTI
LISA		BEN
JOE		JENNIFER
ASHLEY		DAVID
THURSDAY, MARCH 9	12:15 PM (LUNCH RECESS)	
Umpquas	VS.	**Eagles**
JOHN		STEVE
TONY		BILL
LUKE		RYAN
KYLE M.		JEREMY
	12:30 PM	
Callahans	VS.	**Wyldkits**
JASON		HAL
MARK		EBEN
DOUG		GIL
NICK		CHRIS
WEDNESDAY, MARCH 15	1:50 PM	
Rogues	VS.	**Ospreys**
AVERIE		TOM
KYLE P.		AMBER
ALYSSA		SHELLY
CHRIS		SUSIE
	2:05 PM	
Booknights	VS.	**Bookworms**
CHRISTY		JULIE
JON		MATT
ERIC		DANNY
MARGIE		CYNTHIA

Figure 4.2 Reminder Schedule for Teachers

To: _____

Just a Reminder That

_____

_____

_____

_____

_____

Are in the Battle of the Books

Friday_____

at _____

Figure 4.3 Classroom Reminder Notice

Publicity

Do you want to have parties for the winners? Visiting authors at the party? Involve the public library? Arrangements need to be made very early if you are involving people from outside the school.

Do you want publicity in the school and district newsletters? In the community newspaper? On television? If so, prepare news releases and make arrangements for the coverage.

Supplementary Materials

It's nice to have a special bulletin board that can stay up for the duration, and especially good to have if it can be placed in the front hall or another high-visibility area. This board can accommodate sign-up sheets, posters, puzzles about the books, and any other promotional materials. We always post the names of the teams who have signed up for the next battles (see figure 4.4). Pictures of teams and players could also be used. If you choose to have play-offs, the board can be used for tournament charts showing the teams as they progress.

Design special bookmarks to be put in the books being checked out for reading the "Battle" books. These bookmarks give the books more exposure (see figure 4.5).

Team buttons or T-shirts are fun, create a sense of identity for the participants, and—like athletic jackets—enhance the media center's visibility in the school community. Buttons can be made with button makers or be pieces of laminated cardboard (see figure 4.6). Logos

Figure 4.4 Battle Notice for Bulletin Board

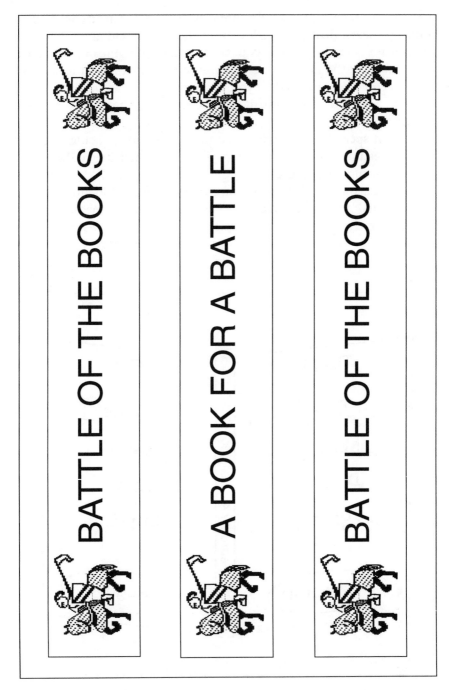

Figure 4.5   Bookmarks

Figure 4.6 Team Badges and Tags

for T-shirts can be made with most computer graphics programs using a special transfer ribbon on a dot-matrix printer. Make sure, if you have writing on the logo, your program will reverse the printing.

"Certificates of Participation" for students or teams can be given out each time a team plays.

Printed invitations for parents and administrators are easy to design and make with computer programs. These should have spaces for filling in the time, date, and names of the teams. They let parents know about a particular child's school activity, and let administrators know what is happening in the library media center (see figure 4.7).

A videotape of the winning teams can be made for the participants. This can also be used as a promotion in the following year. If you want one made, make sure you reserve the camera and a trustworthy photographer well in advance.

Incentives and prizes can increase participation. Local merchants are often willing to donate treats and gift certificates. Bookmarks, bookplates, paper folders, pencils, and stars for the team badges are relatively inexpensive, and can be obtained from library supply companies. Trophies for each building, or trophies that travel to different schools in the district, can be attention getters and these can sometimes be made by recycling old sports trophies. Make sure that you don't let prizes and trophies become ends in themselves; otherwise the fun aspect of the program can be lost. And if you decide to use prizes, you will need to make rules about how the awards are earned—and then make sure that the rules are followed consistently.

Rules

You need to decide on the rules you will use for the contests, and let students know in advance. We usually include these in the book lists we give students. The rules that work for us are these:

1. Any group of four intermediate students may make themselves into a team and challenge any other team by making arrangements with the library staff. Students who sign up for a team must really want to be on that team and should not be signed up without their knowledge by their friends. No changes are made to a team once it has been formed.

BATTLE OF
THE BOOKS

You are
invited to watch
_____
in a playoff,
_____
at _____
_____,
in the Library
Media Center

Figure 4.7 Invitations

2. Each team is made up of four players. If a member is absent, the remaining players play as a team with no substitutes.
3. There are twenty questions to a game.
4. Each team has thirty seconds to come up with the correct answer. They may confer with each other if they wish. During

that thirty seconds they may have as many guesses as they like, and anyone on the team may speak.

5. Questions may be asked about any of the books on the given list, but on no other books.

6. The team receives five points for each correct title given, and three points if they can give the correct name of the author, for a possible total of eight points per question.

7. If, at the end of thirty seconds, the team is unable to answer the question, the opposing team has five seconds in which to give the correct answer. They have only one chance. If they miss, the question goes to the audience.

8. If the first team is able to give the title of the book (and scores five points), but cannot name the author, the opposing team does not have a chance to answer the question.

9. The audience may not coach members of the team, or talk while the battle is going on. When a question is missed by both teams, the audience may answer any part of the question, either author or title, that has not been answered by either team.

10. All students must remain in their seats at all times.

Change these rules as you need to. For example, some schools prefer that each team select a spokesperson who is the only one allowed to give the answer. This minimizes confusion. If you decide to do this, include the fact in the rules you give to students and make sure the rule is enforced with a penalty . . . such as a point subtracted for each answer that does not go through the spokesperson.

Tournaments and Play-offs

It isn't necessary to have play-offs between teams, but they are fun. They do add to the competitive pressure, but also make a good end-of-year activity. There are different ways to set these up. One is by grade level, letting teams from the same grade battle each other until a winner is chosen by elimination. Another is to pick the highest scoring teams, or the ones who have played most often, and let these compete until a school winner is determined. Urbana uses a round-robin type of tournament, with daily matches between teams.[3]

A more complex method is the athletic tournament model, in

which teams are "seeded" according to their average scores. This keeps interest high, as teams which are roughly equivalent in ability progress through a series of "brackets" until a winner is chosen. Seeding keeps the best teams from eliminating each other in early rounds, since they don't meet until the very end.

If you use this method, you will need to have an even number of teams. Don't use more than sixteen, though, or it will take forever! You can have some preliminary play-off battles if it is necessary to eliminate a team or two in order to get down to sixteen.

The next step is to determine the average score for each team by adding up their total scores and dividing by the number of battles they played. Rank each team in descending order (see figure 4.8)

Divide the number of teams in half to get a number which you will use to separate the teams. For example, if you have sixteen teams, this number will be eight. If there are ten teams, the number will be five. This is the number that will be used to match the teams as you place them in brackets (see figures 4.9 and 4.10). This keeps the pairings relatively even.

Teams	Battles			Total Scores	Div. by Total No. of Battles	Final Score	Team Rank
	1	2	3				
Chicarees	111	+97	--	208	208/2	104	1
Gliders	93	+85	+77	255	255/3	85	2
Jousters	77	+55	--	132	132/2	66	3
Rogues	28	+66	+95	189	189/3	63	4
Bookworms	47	+68	+72	187	187/3	62	5
Pages	69	+33	--	102	102/2	51	6
Owls	43	+51	--	94	94/2	47	7
Wyldkits	45	+21	+55	121	121/3	40	8

Figure 4.8 Scores and Team Rankings

Rank	Team Name
1	Chicarees
2	Gliders
3	Jousters
4	Rogues
5	Bookworms
6	Pages
7	Owls
8	Wyldkits
9	Timbertops
10	Ospreys
11	Booknights
12	Umpquas
13	Bobkits
14	Eagles
15	Mountaineers
16	Callahans

Figure 4.9   16 Teams Ranked in
Order of Scores

Rank	Team Name
1	Chicarees
2	Gliders
3	Jousters
4	Rogues
5	Bookworms
6	Pages
7	Owls
8	Wyldkits
9	Timbertops
10	Ospreys

Figure 4.10   10 Teams Ranked in
Order of Scores

Brackets are arranged by putting each pair of teams within a bracket. Begin by working with the odd-numbered teams. Place them in brackets according to the examples in the above figures. Repeat for the even-numbered teams. These examples can be adapted to any number of teams that you have. Eight or sixteen teams work out evenly and make it easy to figure the brackets (see figure 4.11). However, if you keep the method of separating the teams in mind, and follow the example in figures 4.11 and 4.12, you should be able to work out the brackets for any number of teams in the finals.

If you divide the number of teams by the number of battles you plan for a given day, you will come up with the number of days you

1 (Chicarees) vs. 9 (Timbertops)		2 (Gliders) vs. 10 (Ospreys)	
3 (Jousters) vs. 11 (Booknights)		4 (Rogues) vs. 12 (Umpquas)	
5 (Bookworms) vs. 13 (Bobkits)		6 (Pages) vs. 14 (Eagles)	
7 (Owls) vs. 15 (Mountaineers)		8 (Wyldkits) vs. 16 (Callahans)	

Figure 4.11 16 Teams, Paired Off for Brackets

1 (Chicarees) vs. 6 (Pages)	2 (Gliders) vs. 7 (Owls)
3 (Jousters) vs. 8 (Wyldkits)	4 (Rogues) vs. 9 (Timbertops)
5 (Bookworms) vs. 10 (Ospreys)	(Bye)

Figure 4.12 10 Teams, Paired Off for Brackets

will need for the final tournament. With three battles on a given day, the play-offs for sixteen teams will take five days to complete. At three battles a day, the play-offs will take four days to complete.

Arrange the brackets in charts like those in figures 4.13 or 4.14 in order to determine the number of battles that will be required, and the number of days it will take. "Byes" can be used when there are unequal numbers of teams. Another method of handling unequal numbers is to let the losing team with the best score be in the quarter or semi-finals (see the semi-final bracket in figure 4.14).

It's always a fine line between feelings of cooperation, enjoyable competition, and intimidation. Mona Kerby points out the necessity of teaching good sportsmanship and preparing students for losing.[4] You don't want to let the school winners and tournament play-offs become the main focus of the program.

In the original Urbana battles, play-offs between schools were held in the public library. Names of students who had been in school battles were placed in boxes according to grade levels. These names were drawn out so that each team in the final play-off had one fourth-, one fifth-, and one sixth-grade member. This method created new teams and gave the children a chance to learn to work together with others whom they did not necessarily know. Independent schools in Providence, Rhode Island, put students from the competing schools on the same teams in order to foster a spirit of cooperation.[5]

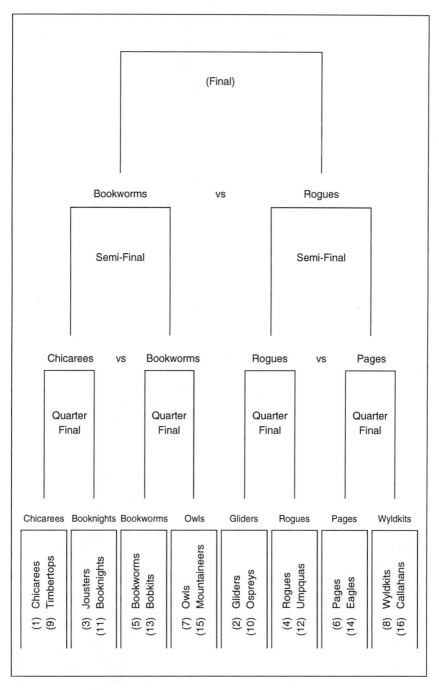

Figure 4.13 A 16-Team Tournament Play-off

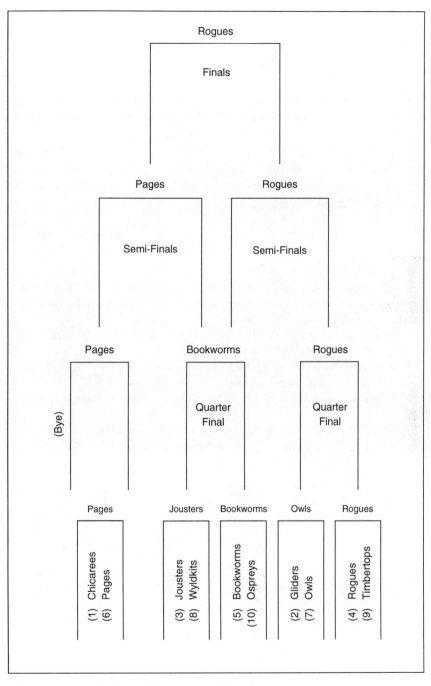

Figure 4.14 A 10-Team Tournament Play-off

Des Plaines has intra-mural play-offs within the district, and follows up with a party in the public library for all the building level winners.

When everything is as prepared as possible, get going and stop worrying. Remember, children are more enthusiastic than critical about projects they truly enjoy.

The main purpose of these book contests is to encourage a love of reading and is just one more way to focus attention on some of the literature in a school library media center collection. If they are to be enjoyable, the activities must foster a feeling of success, not defeat, in every student. We all hope to see our students feel like one of Kerby's, who is quoted as saying to his teacher, "Mrs. E., I finally found something I can do right!"[6]

NOTES

1. Construction paper tears after a few trips through the book drop, but is easily replaceable. If you are into frugal flash, you can cut up mylar potato chip bags. The inside is shiny silver, and can be written on by overhead marking pens. The silver really shows up on a bookshelf.

2. Janet Greeson and Karen Taha, *Name That Book* (Metuchen, New Jersey: Scarecrow Press, 1986), p. 4.

3. Joanne Kelly, *Battle of Books: K-8* (Littleton, Colorado: Teacher Ideas Press, a division of Libraries Unlimited, 1990), pp. 144-45.

4. Mona Kerby, "Battle of the Books," *School Library Journal* (January 1988): 41.

5. Nancy Menaldi-Scanlon, "Cooperation Not Competition Is the Key in Annual 'Battle of the Books,'" *At Wheeler* (newsletter) (June 1991): [2].

6. Kerby, "Battle of the Books," 41.

5

A Timeline for Planning

I t's a good idea to start your preparation several months before you plan to begin. We have suggested this timeline to make sure that all the bases are covered. It is obviously organized on a school schedule, with the battles beginning in January, but can be adapted to suit any situation. Look it over. You may find that you need more or less time to launch the project.

July and August

Read, think, plan. Decide on your goals for the project, and a general idea of how you will begin the program. Choose a format and rules that will work for you. Keep it as simple as possible in the beginning.

September

Introduce the program to the administration and tell them what you hope to do and why. How will you measure its success? Be prepared to answer such questions as "Why should we do this?" and "How will this benefit the kids?"

Follow up at a faculty meeting. Find out who is interested in becoming involved.

Decide on how you will proceed the first year. How many battles? How often?

October

Prepare a suggested book list.

Solicit other suggestions for books from students and teachers.

Choose the questions you will use.

November

Create your final list of books.

Make sure that you have enough copies of the titles to meet your needs. This will depend on the size of the list as well as the number of participants. A small list or large group will need several copies of each title; a large list or small group may need only one or two.

Make a list of rules.

Plan the times and dates for the winter battles.

Plan the dates for the play-offs, and where they will take place.

If other places or people will be involved, make arrangements for these *now*.

December

Sort out questions into groups for different battles.

Print the book lists.

Create a special shelf for the books, or begin marking the books in a special way so they can be identified when on the shelf.

January

Introduce the idea to the students.

Hand out the list of rules.

Hand out the book lists.

Make sure that students know where the books can be found.

Let children begin forming teams.

Arrange for the place where the battles will be held. Make sure you have the necessary chairs, tables, timers, etc.

Prepare score sheets to be used in battles.

Sign-ups for battles may take place.

February

Begin the battles.

You may wish to write up a news release for the school or district newsletter (see figure 5.1).

March

Finish the regular battles.

If you are going to have play-offs, determine who will be in them and when they will take place.

The "Battle of the Books"

In what book does the action take place in the Hundred Aker Wood? In which book does a girl have a long talk with a caterpillar? In which book does Admiral Byrd send a penguin to a house painter? If you can answer these questions you are obviously a bookworm, and are ready for the "Battle of the Books."

This is our fifth year for "Battles" at our school. We have them during the winter months when students have the time to read books thoroughly. All questions are limited to the hundred books on the book list, and the questions are about the story's characters, settings, or plots.

Any four intermediate (4–6) students can form themselves into a team, and we usually have a long list of teams waiting to play. Each team has 30 seconds to answer the questions and gets 5 points for each correct title, plus 3 points for the correct author. If the first team can't come up with the answer, the second team may try. If neither team can answer, the audience has a chance.

We have the battles Friday afternoons from 2:15 to 3 P.M. Come join the fun!

Figure 5.1 Newsletter Article

Tally the scores for the teams and seed them.

Prepare a chart showing when and who will play.

April

Prepare special invitations that students can take home to their parents.

Invite the district administrators to come to watch.

Arrange for the video camera, and any other publicity you may wish to have.

Play-offs begin.

May/June

Have the celebration party.

Return books to the regular collection. Tally any evidence of increased circulation in the books placed on the list.

Gather statistics on student participation, circulation and reading.

As you make plans for the following year, you may wish to survey teachers and students. How can you make it better next year? Solicit suggestions for improvements from all participants: parents, teachers, students, and any others who may have been involved. Their reactions to the project are invaluable in making sure that the program continues to meet their expectations, and justifies your time and effort.

Some of the topics you may wish to cover are: Did the teachers get new ideas for the books they read aloud in class? Do they feel that students improved their leisure reading habits and reading skills? Were there any improvements in scores on standardized tests that might reflect this increase? Did the students find the project fun? Do the students also feel that this program improved their reading ability? Their understanding and knowledge of literature? Their enjoyment of reading?

With all these comments in hand, you should be able to move confidently toward more battles in the years to come. In the words of one student, "This is the funnest thing I have ever done!" May you all feel the same way.

PART

2

The
Questions

101 Dalmations
Smith, Dodie

In what book does the smallest puppy travel in a little blue cart pulled by some bigger ones?

In what book do the dogs get help and send news back and forth by way of the Twilight Barking?

In what book is there a woman who wears a simple white mink cloak? One side of her head has white hair, while the other side has black.

In what book do the dogs roll in soot to turn themselves safely black?

In what book are puppies dognapped so their fur can be used to make a coat?

Abel's Island
Steig, William

In what book does a mouse keep trying to cross a river, using everything from a raft to a catapult?

In what book is a mouse's picnic disrupted by a terrible storm?

In what book does a mouse decide that no one will come to his rescue? If he wants to return home, he will have to figure out a way on his own.

In what book does a mouse find that he doesn't need to pay attention to the time on his watch, but he does need to hear it tick?

In what book does Abelard use bowls rather than bottles to float notes down a river?

Across Five Aprils
Hunt, Irene

What book is about a border state family torn between loyalty to the North and loyalty to the South?

In what book does an angry Union mob burn a barn and put coal oil in the well?

In what book is an Illinois farm boy given trouble because one of his brothers joined the Rebels?

In what book do the "cracker barrel heros" pick on Jethro because he defends a southern soldier?

In what book does Dave Burdow, a family's enemy, protect their youngest son from an attack?

Adam of the Road
Gray, Elizabeth

In what book does the hero first lose his father, and then has his dog stolen by a minstrel and his harp stolen by robbers?

What book is about a boy living in thirteenth-century England?

In what book does a boy fall off a wall while he is watching a biblical play about Adam's fall?

In what book does a young minstrel wander over medieval England looking for his dog and his father?

In what book is a dog named Nick stolen by the minstrel, Jankin?

Adventures of Pinocchio, The
Collodi, Carlo

In what book does the hero acquire donkey ears?

In what book did the hero offer to let himself be burned up in place of his friend, Arlecchino?

In what book is the main character made out of wood?

In what book does a boy's nose grow longer every time he tells a lie?

In what book does a blue fairy play an important part?

Adventures of Tom Sawyer, The
Twain, Mark

In what book did a boy pretend it was such fun white-washing a fence that all his friends begged to have a turn?

In what book do two boys see a murder in the graveyard?

In what book does a boy let himself be whipped in order to protect the girl who actually tore the teacher's book?

In what book is a cave boarded up after some lost children are found? No one knows that the robbers are still in it.

In what book does a boy hope to get punished by the schoolmaster, so he can sit with the girls?

Afternoon of the Elves
Lisle, Janet Taylor

In what book does an eleven-year-old girl secretly take care of her mother all by herself?

In what book does a girl make a tiny village in her backyard?

In what book does a miniature ferris wheel made from two bicycle wheels start turning by itself?

In what book does Hillary almost lose her old friends because of her fascination with the strange girl who lives in the house behind her?

In what book is Sara-Kate teased because she brings only cereal for her school lunch?

Alice's Adventures in Wonderland
Carroll, Lewis

In what book does a blue caterpillar tell a story about Father William?

In what book does a girl find that she can change her size by eating and drinking different things?

In what book does a little girl experience incredibly strange adventures after falling down a rabbit hole?

In what book does a girl swim in the pool of tears that she made by crying?

In what book is there a croquet game using live flamingos and hedgehogs?

All of a Kind Family
Taylor, Sydney

In which book does a mother hide buttons to make sure her daughters do a thorough job of dusting each week?

What book is about five little Jewish sisters?

In which book do the children celebrate the Sabbath, Purim, and Yom Kippur, which is a day of forgiveness?

In which book do the girls look forward to their Friday Library Day?

In which book is the new baby different from the other five children in the family?

Alvin's Secret Code
Hicks, Clifford B.

In which book is a boy known as Secret Agent K 21½?

In which book do two boys ask Mr. Link, a former spy, to teach them about ciphers and code wheels?

In which book does a boy lead an entire town on a hunt for buried treasure?

In which book do two boys find a secret message that says "Serious Milly Hiding Thursday. Start Secrets. Ivan Hiding Message Oak. Remain Silent. Herman"?

In which book does a boy's little sister, whom he calls "the pest," want to be a secret agent, too?

Amazing Memory of Harvey Bean, The
Cone, Molly

In what book does a boy go to school with shoes but no socks?

In what book does a boy spend the summer in a crazy looking house that has an astounding collection of junk?

In what book does a boy befriend a man who collects damaged food from supermarket dumpsters?

In what book is a boy so forgetful that he neglects to tell his separated parents where he is spending the summer?

In what book does a forgetful boy learn to remember things by reciting a simple rhyme that begins with "one is bun, two is shoe, three is tree . . . "?

Amos Fortune, Free Man
Yates, Elizabeth

What book is about a slave who bought his own freedom, then bought freedom for many other slaves?

In what book is a black man lucky because he is bought by a Quaker family who teaches him to read and write?

In what book does a man have to save up his money to buy the woman he wishes to be his wife?

In what book does a slave refuse his independence because he admires his master?

In what book is a young African prince captured by slavers and taken to Boston?

And Condors Danced
Snyder, Zilpha Keatley

In what book does Carley feel she has finally learned how to become invisible?

In what book do firecrackers upset the Presbyterian float during the 4th of July parade?

In what book is Carley spoiled and loved by a Chinese house servant, Woo Ying?

In what book does a dog named Tiger save two children from being bitten by a mad coyote?

In what book does Carley feel awful because she was able to cry terribly when her dog died, yet she couldn't cry when her mother died?

. . . And Now, Miguel
Krumgold, Joseph

In what book does a New Mexico boy fool a ewe into adopting an orphan lamb?

In what book is the family always glad when the Marquez brothers come to shear their sheep?

In what book does a boy try to undo a prayer after it comes true and Gabriel is drafted into the Army?

In what book did Mickey skip school in order to find the family's lost sheep? His grandfather calls him a "real pasTOR."

In what book does a boy pray to San Ysidro that he will be allowed to journey to the Sangre de Cristo Mountains?

Angry Waters
Morey, Walt

In what book is a boy sent to a farm as a condition of his probation?

In what book is a boy arrested for driving a car during a supermarket holdup?

In what book does Dan stand off a calf-killing cougar?

In what book does a boy train the calves Rosie and Beauty?

In what book does a boy's knowledge of motors prove useful in salvaging logs from the Columbia River?

Anne of Green Gables
Montgomery, L. M.

Who breaks her slate over the head of a boy who teases her about her carrot hair?

In what book does a girl refuse to speak to Gilbert for five years—all because he teased her when she first came to the school?

Who is pretending to be the dead Elaine of Astolat as she floats down a river—only to nearly drown when the flatboat springs a leak?

Name one of the books that takes place at a time when orphan children were expected to work for their keep.

Who falls and breaks her ankle, after accepting a dare to walk on the ridge of a roof?

"B" Is for Betsy
Haywood, Carolyn

In what book do the schoolchildren watch Waggle and Wiggle turn into frogs?

In what book did a little girl lose her way to school?

In what book does a little boy carry a dozen eggs to school inside the cap he is wearing—and one breaks while it is on his head?

In what book does a little girl rescue a dog from a deep hole—and receive one of the dog's puppies as a reward?

In what book is there a policeman named Mr. Kilpatrick who helps children cross the street?

Babe; The Gallant Pig
King-Smith, Dick

In which book does an animal keep some rustlers from stealing the sheep?

In which book does a sheepdog named Fly act as a mother to a piglet?

In what book do the sheep start behaving properly once they are asked politely?

In which book does the main character become friends with an old ewe named Ma?

In which book does a piglet learn to behave like a puppy?

Bambi
Salten, Felix

In what book does the old stag call Gobo "a poor thing" because he's been captured and wears a halter around his neck?

In what book does the crow tell the animals about Man, and that Man's third hand is dangerous?

In what book does the main character have two little cousins, Faline and Gobo?

In what book do the hunters kill a little deer's mother and many of his animal friends?

In what book does an old stag save a young one who has been shot?

Bear Called Paddington, A
Bond, Michael

In what book does a bear fall down an escalator?

In what book does the main character love to eat marmalade?

In what book does an animal refuse to stop wearing his bush hat?

In what book does a small animal get lost in a store window display?

In what book is a little animal from darkest Peru named after a railroad station?

Bear's House, The
Sachs, Marilyn

In which book does a ten-year-old girl have no friends at school because she smells and sucks her thumb?

In which book does Fran Ellen sneak away from school at recess time to care for her ten-month-old baby sister?

In which book does Fran Ellen work on her math at home in the evening so that she can spend math time at school sitting by a dollhouse in the back of the room, imagining conversations with the three bears that live inside?

In which book do a ten-year-old girl and her brother and two sisters care for their house and baby sister because their mother has given up after their father disappeared?

In which book does a teacher give a dollhouse to a little girl as a reward for stopping her thumbsucking and not playing hooky?

Beauty
Wallace, Bill

In what book does a boy discover that riding a cattle horse takes different skills from riding a trail horse?

In what book does a boy have to shoot his beloved horse after she gets her legs caught in the cattle guard?

In what book does Luke's mother, usually meek and mild, sock a neighbor because she thinks he's been starving her horse?

In what book does Luke get talked into playing cowboy with the horses even though his grandfather said no?

In what book does a boy's grandfather get his leg caught in the hay baler?

Benjy, the Football Hero
Van Leeuwen, Jean

In what book does the fourth-grade teacher make the kids copy pages from a dictionary when they misbehave?

In what book does Jason use his pet snake to get some advantages from the superstars at the mall?

In what book does a small fourth-grader learn great sports plays by watching the Seattle Seahawks?

In what book does a boy discover that going trick-or-treating with his little sister really pays off in candy?

In what book do the Flannagans beat the Renaldis in the fourth-grade Superbowl?

Big Red
Kjelgaard, Jim

In what book does a trapper's son yearn to own a champion Irish setter that is worth $7,000?

In what book does a rich woman decide not to take her gift dog after he's been sprayed by a skunk?

In what book do a boy and his dog battle with a bear called Old Majesty?

What book takes place in the forests and hills of the Wintapi and Stoney Lonesome?

In what book is Danny trapped on a mountain when his foot is pinned to the ground by a buck's antlers?

Black Beauty
Sewall, Anna

In which book does a horse save his master by refusing to cross a broken bridge?

What book is about a horse who is generally mistreated?

In what book is an old horse recognized by his markings: "white star in the forehead, one white foot on the offside, and a little patch of white hair called a three penny bit"?

In what book does a horse have pleasant memories of his first master, Squire Gordon?

In what book is the author protesting against cruelty to animals, particularly horses?

Black Stallion, The
Farley, Walter

Which book is about a horse who kept a boy from losing his life?

In what book does Alec insist that the ship that rescues him must also rescue his horse?

In which book do a boy and a horse go by ship from India to New York?

In what book do a boy and a horse survive a shipwreck by landing on an uninhabited island?

In what book does a wild stallion finally get to race in the Kentucky Derby?

Blind Connemara, The
Anderson, C. W.

In what book does a girl get a job as a stable hand?

In what book does the horse learn what to do by listening to the sound of Rhonda's voice?

In what book does Rhonda ride her horse all the way to the country fair when her parents' car breaks down?

In what book is Rhonda given the pony of her dreams only after he loses his sight?

In what book does a pony with a handicap become an inspiration for handicapped children?

Blossoms and the Green Phantom, The
Byars, Betsy

In which book is helium the final ingredient for a boy's invention?

In which book does a boy feel he is the only failure in his family because none of his inventions have ever worked?

In which book is the grandfather trapped inside a dumpster with a puppy he tried to rescue?

In which book does a dog named Mud become jealous of a puppy named Dump?

In which book is a boy's invention made of three air mattresses and some garbage bags, painted with fluorescent polka dots?

Blue-Eyed Daisy, A
Rylant, Cynthia

In what book is Ellie the youngest daughter of a coal miner?

In what book does Ellie make cookies as a Christmas gift for James?

In what book does Ellie find she can't shoot a gun after a boy she knows is killed?

In what book does a girl dread Valentine's Day and is glad when the school bus can't get through?

In what book do Ellie's four teenage sisters get her all dolled up for her first boy-girl party?

Book of Three, The
Alexander, Lloyd

In what book does Taran find adventure when Hen Wen the pig runs away?

In what book does a boy live with Dallben, an enchanter, who is 379 years old?

In what book does Eilonwy free Fflewddur Fflam from Aachren's dungeon by mistake?

In what book does the Princess Eilonwy rescue Taran from a dungeon?

In what book is there a hairy character named Gurgi who always wants his "crunchings and munchings"?

Borrowers, The
Norton, Mary

What book is about a family of little people who use items borrowed from humans?

In what book are the main characters named Homily, Pod and Arrietty?

In what book is a house wallpapered with old letters from a wastebasket?

In what book does Pod discover Arrietty is talking with the night boy?

In what book does a housekeeper lock a boy up in the schoolroom while she gets rid of the little people?

Boy Who Spoke Chimp, The
Yolen, Jane

In which book do Kriss and his animal get rescued by an old hermit?

In which book does a boy discover that he can use sign language to talk to some animals?

In which book do a boy and an old man rescue a starving animal from an earthquake-damaged pet store?

In which book does Kriss plan to go camping by himself on his way to his grandmother's?

In what book does Kriss find himself alone with two laboratory apes when the van in which he was riding is destroyed by an earthquake?

Boy Who Wanted a Family, The
Gordon, Shirley

In which book is a boy named Michael bounced around from foster home to foster home?

In which book does a boy named Michael keep all of his belongings in a brown leather suitcase?

In which book does a boy named Michael move in with a lady who keeps a Christmas tree up all year and writes stories for a living?

In which book does a boy's new mom give him a vegetable garden of his own as a birthday present?

In which book does a boy's new mom take him on wonderful Saturday adventures? Instead of grocery shopping and doing household chores, they walk along the beach or spend the day in the desert.

Bridge to Terabithia
Paterson, Katherine

In what book does Jess, who has spent all summer training to become the best runner in fifth grade, find himself beaten by a new girl named Leslie?

In what book do Jess and Leslie use Narnia as the pattern for their own private world?

In what book does a boy's best friend die from falling off a rope into a flooded stream?

In what book is a boy befriended by his music teacher?

After the death of his best friend, in what book does a boy share his own private world with his little sister?

Bristle Face
Ball, Zachary

In what book does a no-good, turtle-chasing dog turn into the leader of the pack of fox hounds?

In which book does a dog love to dig up turtles?

In what book do a runaway dog and a runaway boy find a good home with a storekeeper who is running for sheriff?

In what book is a dog described as looking as if "he had started out to be a hound and then decided he'd look better as a porcupine"?

In what book does a hound dog go blind after chasing the cross fox for thirty hours?

Bronze Bow, The
Speare, Elizabeth

In what book does Samson—a deaf, mute Negro—save Daniel's life?

In what book does the title of the book come from a password used by the band of rebels?

In what book does Daniel decide to become a blacksmith and look after his sister Leah?

In what book do some children pledge themselves to fight the Romans?

In what book is Daniel part of an outlaw band, fighting against the Roman conquerors?

Building Blocks
Voigt, Cynthia

In what book does Brann find himself living thirty-seven years ago, when his father was young?

In what book does Kevin rescue a boy from a cave?

In what book does Brann discover that his friend Kevin is probably his father?

In what book does Brann fall asleep in a wooden block fort in his basement and wake up in a wooden block fort in Kevin's bedroom?

In what book do some blocks made long ago for Brann's father turn out to have special powers?

Bunnicula
Howe, Deborah

Which book is supposedly written by a dog named Harold?

In what book do white vegetables show up in the refrigerator?

In what book does Chester the cat suspect the new pet rabbit must be a vampire?

In what book does a rabbit turn beets and carrots white?

In what book is there a rabbit with strange teeth and cape-like markings on his back?

By the Shores of Silver Lake
Wilder, Laura Ingalls

In what book is Pa a paymaster for the railroad company?

In what book does a family take their first trip on a railroad train?

In what book is a paymaster strung up by the workers who wanted full pay?

In what book does a father find the perfect homestead when he's out chasing wolves?

In what book does Laura watch a railroad being built in the Dakota Territory?

"C" Is for Cupcake
Haywood, Carolyn

In which book does Christy bring her white rabbit to school?

In which book does Chuckie eat almost anything that is brought to school, such as cornflakes, green sugar, and popcorn?

In what book do the children invite their fathers to school for a special breakfast—and then get so excited they forget to cook the food?

In which book does a present melt all over the shelf?

In what book does a Siamese cat named Charlie Cat visit the first grade and prove he is not a careful cat?

Caddie Woodlawn
Brink, Carol Ryrie

In what book does a family vote on whether to go back to England and let their father become a wealthy lord, or whether to stay on the American frontier?

What little girl rode off to warn her Indian friends that the whites were talking about a massacre?

In what book is the heroine given a scalp belt by Indian John?

In what book do some children put on a show for friends, using old birds nests and marbles for admission?

In what book is the heroine encouraged to run freely with her brothers so she will grow up healthy?

Call It Courage
Sperry, Armstrong

In what book is Stout Heart the name of a coward?

In what book is there an albatross named Kivi and a dog named Uri?

In what book does a boy make a knife and an axe out of whale-bones?

In what book does the boy save his dog from a hammerhead shark?

What book is about a boy named Mafatu?

Call of the Wild, The
London, Jack

In which book is a large half shepherd, half St. Bernard dog sold to some shady characters on the docks in Seattle?

In which book does a pampered California dog learn to survive in the uncivilized Alaskan wilderness by fighting, stealing food, and answering to a relentless whip?

In which book does a dog named Buck serve as the lead dog for a mail sled in the Alaskan wilderness?

In which book is a dog named Buck rescued from a fatal beating by a man named John Thornton?

In which book does a dog successfully win a challenge in which his beloved master bets he can pull a sled carrying 1,000 pounds of weight?

Castle in the Attic, The
Winthrop, Elizabeth

In what book does William Edward Lawrence meet Sir Simon of Hargrave?

In what book does William use his gymnastics routine so the wicked wizard will hire him as a fool?

In what book does a boy use a magic token to shrink a special friend?

In what book is there a final battle against Alastor?

In what book does William shrink himself to a small size in order to rescue a friend?

Cat Ate My Gymsuit, The
Danziger, Paula

In what book does Marcy's weight cause her to feel self-conscious?

In what book does Marcy lose her shyness as she becomes involved in a student protest?

What book's title is from an excuse to get out of class?

In what book does the Smedley club help a girl learn to understand her problems?

In what book is Marcy's teacher forced to resign even though she's an excellent teacher?

Cat Who Went to Heaven, The
Coatsworth, Elizabeth

In what book are cats left out of a picture of various animals visiting Buddha?

In which book does a Japanese housekeeper use food money to buy a cat?

In what book is an artist willing to keep a tri-colored cat because they are lucky?

In what book does a priest ask an artist to paint a picture of the death of the Lord Buddha?

In what book is Good Fortune unhappy about being left out of a painting?

Charlie and the Chocolate Factory
Dahl, Roald

In which book does Violet turn into a giant blueberry?

In which book is a a winning candy bar bought with the last of a boy's money?

In which book does a boy's grandfather accompany him on his prize trip through a manufacturing plant?

In what book are the Oompaloompas crazy over cacao beans?

In what book does a boy win a golden ticket for a special trip?

Charlotte's Web
White, E. B.

In which book are the words "radiant," "terrific," and "humble" used to describe a pig and save his life?

In what book does the main character like to eat such things as flies, grasshoppers, and crickets?

In what book does the heroine save the life of a pig?

What book ends with baby spiders floating away?

In what book is there a rat called Templeton and a girl named Fern?

Children of the Dust Bowl
Stanley, Jerry

What book tells how families left their farms and traveled in broken-down cars to California where there was supposed to be work?

In what book do the blowing winds create so much static electricity that the wild jackrabbits are electrocuted?

In what book does Patsy cry when she sees the green valleys of California?

In what book are children thought to be stupid because they are so poor that they only have coffee grounds and carrot stems to eat?

In what book do children and teachers build their own school including an airport runway and a swimming pool?

Chitty Chitty Bang Bang
Fleming, Ian

In what book does Commander Crackpot make magic whistling candy?

In what book will you find an amazingly versatile car?

In which book are the children's names Jeremy, Mimsy and Jemima?

In what book is the "Paragon Panther" rescued by Commander Crackpot?

In what book is there a character named Commander Caractacus Pott?

Computer Nut, The
Byars, Betsy

In what book is there a character who comes from the planet Bagel?

In what book did a girl find mysterious messages on her father's computer screen?

In what book does an alien try to tell funny jokes?

Who found herself typing messages to something or someone called BB-9?

In what book does an alien take on human form?

Cowboy Boots
Garst, Shannon

In what book does Bob save a girl from drowning by the use of his roping ability?

In what book does Bob name his pony "Boots"?

In what book does Bob have to really work hard at proving himself a cowboy?

In which book does Bob help his friend Montana break a horse called Dynamite?

In which book does a boy expect to be a real cowboy when he goes to his uncle's ranch?

Cricket in Times Square, The
Selden, George

In which book does Chester eat a $2 bill from the Bellini's cash register?

In what book does a pet insect become a newspaper stand attraction?

In what book are the characters a mouse, an insect, and a cat named Harry?

In what book does an insect learn to play human music by listening to the radio?

Which book is about a pet insect named Chester kept by a newsboy named Mario?

Cybil War, The
Byars, Betsy

What book is about two boys who both like the same girl?

In what book does a girl like peanut butter-covered carrots?

In what book does the class play cast Tony as a dill pickle, Simon as a jar of peanuts, and the heroine as Ms. Indigestion?

In what book does Simon put a pirate costume on his dog T. Bone?

In what book is Simon tricked into going on a date with Harriet?

Danger in Quicksand Swamp
Wallace, Bill

In what book do two boys find a canoe buried in the sand?

In what book are some boys marooned on an island that is surrounded by alligators?

In what book does Ben use his blue jeans and belt to save Jake's life?

In what book do two boys trap a murderer in thick loose sand?

In what book does Lisa find a cork doll and a treasure map in Ben's secret hiding place? Later on, she uses her knowledge to save Ben's life.

Daniel Boone
Daugherty, James

What book is about a famous frontiersman who kept moving west? His name is the title of this book.

In what book did a man talk the Cherokee Indians into selling their hunting grounds to a real estate company?

Which book is about a real man who fought the French along with Major George Washington, fought and was captured by the Indians, and led the grandparents of Abraham Lincoln down the Wilderness Road to Kentucky?

As a young man, he marched along with George Washington under the command of a British general. His name is the title of this book. What is it?

Who spent two years hunting in the wilderness of Kentucky and was robbed of everything by an Indian war party?

Danny Dunn and the Homework Machine
Williams, Jay

In what book do a boy and his friends do their schoolwork on a borrowed computer?

In what book is a computer nicknamed "Miniac"?

In what book does a boy cause a computer to malfunction by tampering with the temperature controls?

In what book do some kids find out that using a computer for their schoolwork is harder than they thought?

In what book does Eddie Phillips foul up the professor's computer?

Danny the Champion of the World
Dahl, Roald

Who lives with his father in an old gypsy caravan behind a filling station?

In what book does a boy help his father illegally hunt for pheasants?

In what book are plump raisins used as the main ingredient in both the "horsehair stopper" and the "sticky hat"?

In what book are some drunken birds hidden in a baby carriage?

In what book does the nine-year-old main character leave in the middle of the night to find his father?

Dark-Thirty: Southern Tales of the Supernatural, The
McKissack, Patricia

In what book does a mother decide to live with the sasquatch colony that has saved her little boy's life?

In what book does a little girl visit a "conjure woman" to ask for a new baby brother?

In what book does a slave family turn into birds and fly away to freedom?

In what book does a woman with a sick baby haunt a bus route every winter until she gets a ride?

In what book does a little girl believe that a monster lives in her grandparents' chicken coop?

Dealing with Dragons
Wrede, Patricia

In what book does a princess volunteer to work for a dragon?

In what book does Cimerone tire of attempted rescues by knights and princes?

In what book does a princess talk a jinn into returning to his bottle for another eighty-three years?

In what book do two girls discover that wizards melt in soap and water?

In what book does a princess find that her knowledge of Latin and ability to make cherries jubilee are very helpful?

Dear Mr. Henshaw
Cleary, Beverly

What book is made up of letters written to an author?

In what book does Leigh get to meet a famous author?

In what book does Leigh write to an author about a book called "Ways to Amuse a Dog"?

In what book does Leigh invent a burglar alarm for his lunch box?

In what book does a boy get a letter from an author asking Leigh to answer ten questions about himself?

Dicey's Song
Voigt, Cynthia

In what book does a girl talk a storekeeper into letting her clean up the store for a dollar an hour so that she can give allowances to her brothers and sisters?

In what book does Sammy fight because he's teased about his grandmother?

In what book do Gram and the children figure out different methods to help Maybeth learn?

In what book does a girl write a composition about her mother that is so well written the teacher reads it aloud as an example of plagiarism?

In what book do two girls discuss how you choose friends? "By what's important to us? Like whether someone's brave or not"?

Did You Carry the Flag Today, Charlie?
Caudill, Rebecca

In what book does Charlie start school and is amazed by running water, blue soap and paper towels?

In what book does a boy wear his uncle's hat to school all day and won't take it off, even when the principal asks him to, because he thinks it's magic?

In what book is a boy missing his two front teeth because he wanted to find out how an apple is attached to the limb of a tree?

In what book does Charlie's curiosity get him into trouble at school?

In what book does Charlie reshelve the library books so their spines are against the wall?

Dollhouse Murders, The
Wright, Betty Ren

In what book does Amy fall in love with an old dollhouse?

In what book does Amy discover the secret of her grandparents' death?

In what book does Aunt Clare admit she's sure it was her fiancé who killed her parents?

In what book do Amy's two sisters find the answer to a murder in a letter that was hidden in a book?

In what book is Louann given Aunt Clare's toy house?

Door in the Wall, The
De Angeli, Marguerite

In what book does a boy on crutches manage to escape from a castle, climb down a ravine, and swim across two rivers?

In what book does Brother Matthew teach Robin how to use wood-carving tools?

In what book is Robin called "Crookshanks" because of his paralyzed legs?

In what book is a crippled boy rescued by a knight?

In what book is Robin, a crippled boy, deserted by his servants?

Dragonsong
McCaffrey, Anne

In what book do the harpers use ballads to give instruction in history?

In what book does Menolly long to be a harper—but her father won't let her become one because she is a girl?

In what book does Menolly find and impress some fire lizards?

In what book do people ride dragons and go "between time"?

What book is set on a planet similar to earth except that burning thread falls from the sky?

Edith Herself
Howard, Ellen

In what book does Edie go to live with her sister Alena after her mother dies?

In what book does Edie want to go to school, but is afraid she'll have one of her fits?

In what book does Edie's brother-in-law squish the baby mice that Edie's found?

In what book is a girl kept from going to school because she has epilepsy and sometimes loses consciousness?

In what book is a girl helped by her nephew and best friend?

Endless Steppe, The
Hautzig, Esther

What book is about a Polish family that is deported to Siberia to work in a gypsum mine?

In what book does the main character cut off her long hair, so that she will be accepted by Svetlana and the other children?

What book is based on the author's life as a ten-year-old child in Siberia?

In what book did a girl use yarn from an old skirt to knit a new sweater?

In what book do Mother and Grandmother work with dynamite while Father drives a horse and cart?

Enormous Egg, The
Butterworth, Oliver

In what book does a boy mount a campaign to save a triceratops from being killed?

In what book does a boy's pet weigh 798 pounds by the end of August?

In what book does a hen have an egg that is too big for her to handle by herself?

In what book does a senator use Nathan's pet as an example of the government wasting taxpayers' money?

In what book does a suitcase manufacturer offer money for Uncle Beazley's hide?

Escape to Witch Mountain
Key, Alexander

In what book are two aliens sent to a detention home for orphans?

In what book is there a little girl named Tia who can only communicate with her brother through ultrasonic speech?

In which book is there a little girl who can't talk but can easily open locked doors?

In what book does Tony have the ability to play a harmonica and make dolls come alive?

In which book do Tony and Tia wonder about their original home?

Explorer of Barkham Street, The
Stolz, Mary

In what book does Martin find that he doesn't need to daydream anymore because he is gradually making friends of his own?

In what book does Martin discover his dog Rufus has almost forgotten him?

In what book does Martin discover that babysitting Ryan is a fun job that pays well?

In what book does Martin daydream about being an explorer at the North Pole?

In what book does the Hastings' family life improve when Martin's grandfather comes to live with them?

Fledgling, The
Langton, Jane

In what book does Georgie believe she can fly? She really can when she uses her magic feather.

In what book does Madeline Prawn think that Georgie must be from fairyland and not a real girl?

In what book is a girl shot by Ralph Preek who mistakes her for a goose?

In what book does a goose teach Georgie how to fly?

In what book does Georgie get a blue and white ball from a bird as a present? The ball glows and becomes the mirror of the earth.

Freaky Friday
Rodgers, Mary

In what book does Annabelle find herself going to a teacher conference about her own behavior—since she now looks like her mother?

In which book does Annabelle find out what her teachers really think about her?

In what book does Annabelle find herself having to behave exactly like her mother?

In what book do a girl and her mother suddenly find themselves involuntarily trading places?

In what book does Annabelle find out that her little brother, Ape Face, really loves her?

From the Mixed Up Files of Mrs. Basil E. Frankweiler
Konigsburg, E. L.

In which book do Claudia and Jamie solve a mystery about a statue they call "Angel"?

In which book do Claudia and Jamie collect money from a museum fountain during the night so they can buy food during the day?

In which book does a girl run away from home because she thinks it will teach her family a lesson in "Claudia Appreciation"?

In what book do Claudia and Jamie find out that a museum statue was carved by the greatest sculptor of all—Michelangelo?

In what book do a brother and sister run away from home and choose to hide in an art museum?

Gathering of Days, A
Blos, Joan

What book is supposedly the diary of thirteen-year-old Catherine Hall?

In what book does a gift of some lace tell a girl that a runaway slave is free?

Which book is supposedly written by Catherine Hall, aged thirteen years, seven months, eight days, of Meredith in the state of New Hampshire?

In which book does Catherine's new stepmother teach her how to quilt?

In what book is Catherine's journal written during the years of 1830–1832?

Gentle Ben
Morey, Walt

In which book do some men with a scythe attack a chained bear—and when he fights back, they decide he's a dangerous animal and should be shot?

In what book does a bear save Mark's family from some fish pirates?

In what book do some characters have descriptive names such as Fog Benson and Mud Hole Jones?

In what book does a boy have a pet Alaskan brown bear?

In which book does a family hide a bear from a hunter named Mud Hole Jones?

Getting Something on Maggie Marmelstein
Sharmat, Marjorie

In what book is there a recipe for a delicious bread pudding at the very end?

In what book do the seventh-graders put on a play about a princess and a frog?

In what book does Thaddeus discover that Mouse Maggie writes love letters to movie stars?

In what book does Thaddeus refer to his project as a G.S.O.M.M. project?

In what book is Gideon Smith the Fifth afraid of being teased about his name?

Ginger Pye
Estes, Eleanor

In what book does Rachel pretend to give a sermon in the church?

In what book does three-year-old "Uncle Benny" find the family's lost dog?

In what book do Rachel and Jerry take a job dusting a church to earn enough money to buy a dog?

In what book does a three-year-old boy find a kidnapped dog and bring it home?

In what book do Jerry and Rachel call the man in a yellow hat an "unsavory character"?

Girl Called Boy, A
Hurmence, Belinda

In what book is a girl bored with hearing tales of her family's slave past and is sure she would have never been one?

In what book does Blanche's father carry an old soapstone lucky charm that he calls the "Freedom Bird"?

In what book does a girl teach her friends how to write even though it's against the law?

In what book does a girl find herself living with a slave family back in the year 1853?

In what book does a girl find that she's thought to be a boy and is living on a long-ago plantation at the time of her great-great-grand-parents?

Give Us a Great Big Smile Rosy Cole
Greenwald, Sheila

In what book does Uncle Ralph want to write a book about his niece's secret talent, only she doesn't have one?

In what book does a girl have to take violin lessons so that she can become the star of a book?

In what book do the neighbors think a family must be using an electric saw in their apartment—but it's only their daughter practicing her violin?

In what book does a girl get people to sign a petition stating she should not take violin lessons?

In what book does a little girl have an uncle who does photo stories on children who are superachievers?

Gloomy Gus
Morey, Walt

Which book title is a slang term for someone who has more troubles than he can handle?

In what book does Eric's bear become a tourist attraction for Tartouche?

In what book is Eric relieved to find that the man who has raised him is not really his father?

In what book does a boy take his bear and run away from a circus?

In what book does a runaway travel the Oregon roads, trying to get to Portland and then to Alaska?

Golden Mare, The
Corbin, William

In what book does a boy cope with the impending death of his palomino by telling a story of a white stallion who comes for her?

In what book does Robin shoot a cougar?

In which book does a sickly boy ride through the snow to get help for his mother who has broken her leg?

In which book does a cowboy named Old Clint promise that a horse called Magic will never die?

In which book does Robin's rheumatic fever keep him from taking part in the usual ranch activities?

Golden Name Day, The
Lindquist, Jennie

In what book are the Swedish holidays as much a part of the story as the American ones?

In what book does Wanda give Nancy her own special day?

In what book does Nancy want a Swedish name?

In what book does Nancy learn about Swedish customs?

In what book does Nancy despair because her name is not a Swedish one?

Great Brain, The
Fitzgerald, John D.

In what book is Tom hired to teach a Greek boy how to fight?

What book is about a boy named Tom who likes to swindle people?

In which book does Tom rescue the Jensen boys from Skeleton Cave?

In what book does JD try to get the mumps on purpose?

Who charges admission to see the first indoor plumbing in town? His nickname is the title of this book.

Great Rescue Operation, The
Van Leeuwen, Jean

In what book do Raymond and Marvin ride a subway across a city to find their missing friend, Fats?

In what book does mouse "Merciless Marvin the Magnificent" fly on a kite?

What book is about a group of mice living in a store's toy department?

In what book is a mouse happy living with a dentist, because he gets all the sweets people aren't allowed to eat?

In what book is a mouse named Fats accidently acquired when a doll carriage is purchased?

Grey Cloud
Graeber, Charlotte Towner

In what book does Tom find an injured pigeon in the field?

In what book do some boys from school badger Tom into driving the old pickup, even though he's underage?

In what book does a boy have to drive a truck to save his friend's life even though he's never driven before?

In what book does Tom's carelessness cost the life of two of Orville's pets?

In what book does Tom help a boy with the farm chores so he can learn how to care for and train some birds?

Grey King, The
Cooper, Susan

In what book does the sound of a golden harp waken the six sleepers to fight against the dark forces?

In what book is Bran really the son of King Arthur?

In what book is a dog with silver eyes able to see the wind and the gales?

In what book is Will the last of the "Old Ones," in the service of the Light?

In what book does Jenny actually turn out to be Queen Guinevere?

Half Magic
Eager, Edward

In which book does Jane find a magic coin which makes wishes come partly true?

In what book does Mark wish himself on a desert island—and finds himself on a desert instead?

In what book does Martha make the cat half talk, and Mark make an iron dog half alive?

In what book does modern Katherine fight and defeat Sir Lancelot?

In what book does a magic charm cause a mother to feel she's lost her mind?

Harriet the Spy
Fitzhugh, Louise

In what book is the main character left out from the sixth-graders' "Spy Catchers Club"?

What book is about a girl with a nursemaid named "Ole Golly" and a friend called "Sport"?

In what book does a heroine carry a flashlight, a notebook, a pen pouch, a canteen, and a Boy Scout knife on her tool belt?

In what book does the principal decide to make the heroine the editor of the sixth-grade page in the newspaper?

In what book does a girl write down every single thing that she sees people doing?

Hatchet
Paulsen, Gary

In what book does a boy survive attacks by a porcupine, a skunk, and a moose?

In what book does a pilot die from a heart attack, leaving a thirteen-year-old boy to fly the plane?

In what book does a boy find that feeling sorry for himself is no help, but patience is absolutely necessary for survival?

In what book does Brian first survive on cherries and raspberries, and then learns to spear fish and hunt "fool birds"?

His English teacher told the kids to look at everything and think of themselves as being their most valuable asset. In which book did a boy put that advice to good use?

Haunt Fox
Kjelgaard, Jim

In what book does a man trap pregnant animals, intending to collect a bounty on all the cubs after they are born?

In what book does an animal finally defeat his old enemy, Stub the wild cat, but only because his mare Vixen comes to his aid?

In what book does Star learn how to spring all Dade Marson's traps?

In what book does Jack finally find the animal he and Thunder have been hunting, but the animal is caught in a trap? Jack sets him free.

In what book does an animal named Star delight in having the dogs chase him because he knows he can outtrick them all?

Heidi
Spyri, Johanna

In what book is a little orphan taken to live with her grandfather, an old hermit who likes living by himself?

In what book does a little girl delight in helping Peter herd the goats Snowflake, Little Swan, and Turk?

In what book does a little girl go to Vienna to be a companion to Clara, a girl who is ill?

What book is about life in the Alps with an old man called Alm-Uncle?

In what book does Peter destroy a wheelchair because he is jealous? Much to his surprise, it turns out to be a good thing for its owner.

Hello, Mrs. Piggle Wiggle
MacDonald, Betty

In what book do Melody's eyes gush enough tears to flood the school yard?

In what book does a special powder make children invisible at certain times?

In what book does a magic spray cure a family of their slowness?

What book tells about candy whisper sticks?

In what book is a bully given some leadership pills?

Hello, My Name Is Scrambled Eggs
Gilson, Jamie

In what book does Harvey try to teach English to a Vietnamese boy?

In what book are name tags used to teach a boy the English name of things?

In what book is Harvey excited over his family's sponsorship of a new boy from Vietnam?

In what book does Tom get an A on a math test, even though he writes the numbers the Vietnamese way?

In what book does Tom decide to keep his own name of Tuan?

Henry Huggins
Cleary, Beverly

In what book does a boy catch night crawlers to earn money for a football?

Who tries to carry his dog on a bus inside a paper bag?

In what book do two guppies keep multiplying until there are fruit jars full of guppies on the dresser, the night table, and all around the walls of the bedroom?

In what book does a dog spill green paint—which saves his owner from being "Little Boy" in the Christmas play?

In what book does a boy hope that talcum powder will make his dog's spots outstandingly white for the dog show but it turns out that he's used pink talcum powder?

Henry Reed, Inc.
Robertson, Keith

In what book does a boy have an adopted beagle named Agony?

In what book do some kids drill for oil and find it? It's in a forgotten fuel tank.

In what book does a beagle have problems trying to catch Midge's pet rabbit?

What book takes place in Grovers Corners, New Jersey?

Hero and the Crown, The
McKinley, Robin

In what book does Aerin use the red jewel made of dragon blood to defeat her wicked uncle?

In what book does Aerin discover an ointment that protects against dragon fire?

In what book does Aerin defeat Maur, the Black Dragon?

In what book does Aerin feel inferior because she is the only royal that doesn't possess magic powers?

What book takes place in the imaginary land of Damar?

High King, The
Alexander, Lloyd

In what book does Taran finally defeat Arawn, Lord of Annuvin, Land of the Dead?

In what book does Taran search for Gwydion's stolen enchanted sword?

In what book does Taran, the assistant pigkeeper, finally become the ruler?

In what book do the wolves free Eilonwy and Gurgi?

In what book does a princess give up her enchanted powers in return for love?

Hobbit, The
Tolkien, J. R.

In what book is there a dragon named Smaug?

Who would you be if your name was Bilbo Baggins and you lived in a nice round hole in a hill?

In what book is there a great beekeeper named Beorn who can change his skin and become a huge black bear?

In what book do Bilbo and Gollum ask riddles?

In what book do some spiders web-wrap some dwarves for dinner?

Homecoming
Voigt, Cynthia

In what book does a mother leave her children alone in a parked car in a shopping center?

In what book does Dicey wash windows in a gas station so she can get a map of Connecticut?

In what book do Sammy and James each tell a lie to help their family—and then Stewart points out that they've really only hurt themselves?

In what book do the children find their aunt has died and their cousin Eunice wants to send them to foster homes?

In what book does a girl manage to take her brothers and sisters to their aunt's house, even though they have been left alone with almost no money?

Homer Price
McCloskey, Robert

In what book does a doughnut machine get stuck and turn out thousands of doughnuts?

Who captures some robbers with the aid of his pet skunk, Aroma?

In what book does a man invent a musical mousetrap and promise to remove all the mice from a town for only $30?

In what book is there a sign offering a $100 prize for finding a bracelet inside a doughnut?

In what book is there a string-saving contest at the county fair?

How to Eat Fried Worms
Rockwell, Thomas

In what book did a boy feel sick every time he thought about the bet he'd made with his friends?

In what book did a boy's mother put item number 11 in an ice-cream cake?

In what book do Alan and Joe stuff Billy with all kinds of junk food, hoping he'll forget about keeping his end of the bet?

In what book did two boys forge a letter from a doctor warning about the danger of pesticides in worms?

In what book do you find descriptions of such food as "Whizbang Worm Delight" and "Worm and Egg on Rye"?

Ida Early Comes over the Mountain
Burch, Robert

In what book does a woman lasso a bear in the school's Wild West program?

In what book do Aunt Myrtle and Aunt Earnestine disapprove of the new housekeeper?

In what book does a woman tell fantastic tall tales aboout her past as a lion tamer, mustang rider, and rope twirler?

In what book does a woman manage to get everyone else to make the stew for her while she plays games?

In what book does a woman believe that reading the funny papers should be done before the dishes?

In the Year of the Boar and Jackie Robinson
Lord, Bette

In what book is there a Chinese girl who doesn't understand the Pledge of Allegiance? She thinks it ends with "little tea and just rice for all."

In what book does Bandit have her name changed to Shirley Temple?

What book begins, "In the year of the Dog, 4645"?

In what book does Shirley keep quiet about how she got her two black eyes?

What book is about a little girl from China who comes to live in New York?

Incredible Journey, The
Burnford, Sheila

Which book is about Tao, the Siamese; Luath, the Labrador; and Bodger, the old Bull Terrier?

In which book is an Indian woman sure she has seen a good omen—the White Dog of the Ojibways has given meat to a cat?

In which book does a Siamese use a rabbit burrow to escape from a lynx?

In which book does a cat save an old bull terrier from a mother bear and her cub?

In which book do the Hunters and Longridges realize that their lost animals must be traveling on a straight route westward?

Indian in the Cupboard, The
Banks, Lynn Reid

In what book does an old cabinet make plastic toys come to life?

In what book do Omri and Patrick let the Indians return to their own time?

In what book does a boy learn to let his toys work out their own destiny?

In what book is a boy given an old plastic man for a birthday present?

Which book is about a boy named Omri?

Invincible Louisa
Meigs, Cornelia

Which book is a biography of the author of *Little Women?*

In what book does a child nearly drown in the frog pond in the Boston Common?

In what book does the heroine get typhoid fever from nursing the soldiers during the Civil War?

In what book does someone predict that a girl will never become a writer? She later becomes a famous author.

In what book does a little girl find a slave hiding in the Dutch oven?

Ishkabibble
Crayder, Dorothy

In what book does Lucy feel she's the class Public Victim #1—with everyone picking on her?

In what book does Lucy finally defeat the three T's?

In what book does Luce the Goose knock down Norton the Tough?

In what book does Lucy find her guru—an old lady with warts on her nose?

In what book does Lucy finally get a magic word that seems to help?

Island of the Blue Dolphins
O'Dell, Scott

In what book is a young girl led back to her home by dolphins?

In what book does a wild dog become Rontu, a girl's companion?

In what book is Karana's brother killed by a pack of wild dogs?

In what book does a girl spend eighteen years alone on an island?

In what book does a girl go to a bluff so she can watch for strangers?

Island of the Loons, The
Hyde, Dayton

In what book does orphaned Jimmy own his own old fishing tug, the Alyce?

In what book does a boy rescue an escaped convict from a shipwreck and the man takes him prisoner instead?

In what book is Jimmy given the last name of the Michigan town which feels it adopted him?

In what book does an escaped convict become an enthusiastic bird-watcher?

In what book do a man and a boy build a cabin and spend a winter on a deserted island?

It's Like This, Cat
Neville, Emily

In which book does Dave befriend a "crazy" lady who feeds him cottage cheese every time he comes to visit?

In which book do Dave and Nick take a cat on an outing to the beach at Coney Island?

In which book does a boy named Dave risk his life on a freeway chasing his pet who jumped out of the car window?

In which book does Dave's pet catch and kill a salamander that Ben was using for a science project?

In which book does a boy's friend, Crazy Kate, inherit a million dollars when her only brother, whom she hasn't seen for over twenty years, suddenly dies?

James and the Giant Peach
Dahl, Roald

In what book does a boy trip and scatter the bag of little green things around an old fruit tree in the garden?

In what book does a boy live with Aunts Spiker and Sponge on the top of a very high hill in England?

In what book does a boy go through a tunnel and find a group of giant garden pests?

In what book is a gigantic fruit speared by the top of the Empire State Building?

In what book are 501 seagulls caught by an earthworm used as bait?

Jeremy Thatcher, Dragon Hatcher
Coville, Bruce

In what book does a dragonlet choose the Babylonian name of Tiamet?

In what book does a pet animal eat chicken livers and drink gallons of milk?

In what book does a librarian use bits of eggshell, baby teeth, and the skin an animal has shed to make a gateway into another world?

In what book does a boy stumble into a magic shop run by S. Elives?

In what book is a boy who loves to draw always in trouble with his art teacher?

John F. Kennedy and P.T. 109
Tregaskis, Richard

In what book do some small Navy boats challenge some destroyers nicknamed "The Tokyo Express"?

In what book does his heroism cause a young lieutenant to lose twenty-five pounds, get sick with malaria, develop a bad back, and become mentally and physically exhausted?

In what book does a man (who later becomes president) rescue the crew of his ship?

In what book does the skipper use his teeth to tow a wounded man to a safe island near the Ferguson Passage?

In which book is a young naval officer and crew rammed by a Japanese destroyer?

Johnny Tremain
Forbes, Esther

In which book is a boy's hand burned severely when a pot of molten silver breaks?

In which book does a boy belong to the "Sons of Victory"?

In which book does a boy carry secret messages to the Boston Patriots?

In what book is there a horse named Goblin?

In what book does a rebel Yankee boy carry messages for the British?

Journey to an 800 Number
Konigsburg, E. L.

In which book does a boy's father own a camel named Ahmed?

In which book does a boy spend a month with a camel keeper, while his mother is away on a honeymoon cruise with her new husband?

In which book does a boy travel with his father and a camel, going to shopping malls, conventions, state fairs, dude ranches and night clubs?

In which book is a baby given the name of Rainbow because his father promised to name him according to an old Indian custom?

In which book does a boy meet a girl and her mother several times, under several names, and under several circumstances, while traveling to conventions with his father?

Journey to Topaz
Uchida, Yoshiko

In what book does President Franklin Roosevelt order all people of Japanese descent to leave their homes?

In what book does Yuki's family have to live in a horse's stall—which the government says is an apartment?

In what book does a family have to go to an internment camp because they are of Japanese origin?

In what book does Ken have to decide about joining the special Nissei unit in the U.S. Army—when the U.S. government has treated him like an enemy?

What book is based on the author's life as a child in a United States internment camp?

Joyful Noise: Poems for Two Voices
Fleischman, Paul

What book is meant to be read aloud by two people at once?

What book tells about book lice in love?

In what book do waterbugs twirl and swirl?

What book tells about fireflies and mayflies, moths and cicadas?

In what book is there a whole poem devoted to a cricket?

Julie of the Wolves
George, Jean

In what book does a girl persuade some wolves to take her in as part of their family?

In what book does a thirteen-year-old girl cross the Alaskan tundra on foot?

In what book does a girl act submissive, so that Amaroq will adopt her?

In what book does a girl use her Eskimo skills to help her survive alone?

In what book does a girl have two names: an Eskimo name and an English one?

Just As Long As We're Together
Blume, Judy

In what book does Stephanie find out that her new friend's mother is really a famous TV star?

In what book is Alison, a new Vietnamese girl, the most popular girl in the fifth grade?

In what book does Stephanie find out that it's okay to be a gullible optimist?

In what book does Stephanie find out that it is hard to be best friends with people who keep secrets?

In what book is a girl surprised to find out that her parents have separated without telling her?

Katie John
Calhoun, Mary

In what book does the heroine have to have a mud bath to get unstuck?

Who promises her family that she will do the hated housework if only they can stay in Missouri instead of going back to California?

In what book did the heroine throw rotten eggs at the old hen—which made a stinky mess in the backyard?

In what book does the heroine find out that the noises she thought were made by a ghost were really made by an old pipe in her house?

In what book does the heroine get trapped on a dumbwaiter?

Kid in the Red Jacket, The
Park, Barbara

In what book does a boy worry about moving to Massachusetts?

In what book does a boy try hard not to be friends with Molly Vera Thompson?

In what book does a boy find out that you have to be considered to be a little bad in order to make friends in a new town?

In what book does Howard discover that it's okay to be friends with a first-grade girl even though they don't like doing the same things?

In what book is a boy given a "watch doll" named Madeline?

King of the Wind
Henry, Marguerite

In what book did a boy named Agba take care of an Arabian stallion named Sham?

In what book is the horse named for the sun?

In what book are six stallions and six slave boys sent as a gift to the Court of Versailles?

In which book does a boy feed camel's milk to a small colt?

In which book does a stallion watch his three sons race to win the queen's plate?

Konrad
Nostlinger, Christine

In what book does a boy arrive inside a can?

In what book are a boy's first clothes: red-and-white-checked underpants, purple corduroy pants with green heart-shaped patches, a T-shirt with spangles, and a blue cap with a golden bell?

In what book is a child who is programmed to be perfect sent to a woman who makes rugs for a living?

In what book did Mrs. Bertolotti order a memory aid, but the factory sends a seven-year-old child instead?

In what book does a woman pour a special nutrient solution over a strange arrival—and it turns into a seven-year-old child?

Lacy Makes a Match
Beatty, Patricia

In what book does a girl encourage her brother to marry an actress who walks on the ceiling?

In what book does an orphan girl track down her parentage through her baby bonnet and dress?

In what book does a girl try to marry off her brothers so that she won't have to do so much housework?

In what book does a girl send off fake letters as she tries to find wives for her brothers?

In what book does a girl get her head stuck in a box while helping a stage magician?

Lassie Come Home
Knight, Eric

In what book does a duke's granddaughter allow a homesick dog to escape?

In what book is a dog taken in by an old couple who care for it, love it, and let it go when it is ready to continue its journey?

In what book does a collie manage to find her way home from Scotland?

In what book is a boy's dog sold to a rich man after the boy's father loses his job in a mine?

In which book does a collie fight a weasel for his food?

Legend of Jimmy Spoon, The
Gregory, Kristiana

In what book does a boy resent having to work in his father's store just because he is the only son?

In what book does a Mormon boy decide to go off with the Indians so he can get a horse?

In what book is a white boy adopted by the chief's old mother?

In what book does a boy steal a feather from an eagle without doing the bird any harm?

In what book does a white boy scare off a grizzly bear, saving the life of a Shoshoni girl?

Letters to Horseface
Monjo, F. N.

What book is made up of letters to a sister, Nannerli?

In what book does a thirteen-year-old boy conduct a symphony, improvise a sonata, and play a violin—all in one concert?

In what book is Wolferl made a Knight of the Order of the Golden Spur?

In what book does a boy copy down all the notes to a long psalm from memory?

In what book does Mozart travel from Vienna to Rome?

Like Jake and Me
Jukes, Mavis

In which book does a boy feel he does not have much in common with his stepfather?

In which book does a boy's mother grow two pears inside a bottle stuck on the end of a branch of a pear tree?

In which book does a boy spot a wolf spider on the back of his stepfather's neck?

In which book does a boy discover that his big, strong, tough stepfather is afraid of spiders?

In which book does the search for a wolf spider inside his stepfather's clothing help to bring a boy and his stepfather closer together?

Limerick Trick, The
Corbett, Scott

Who found himself saying such things as "honest nurse, I talk in verse and all the time it's getting worse"?

In what book does Kirby find himself saying everything in rhyme, without meaning to?

In what book does Kirby use his magic chemistry set to help him write a poem?

In what book do Kirby's rhyming responses get him in trouble?

In what book does Kirby feel a buzzing in his head just before he speaks in verse?

Lincoln: A Photobiography
Freedman, Russell

In what book can you see a photograph of a president's own copybook?

In what book does a man save a newspaper clipping which refers to him as a man of "grand simplicity of purpose and patriotism which . . . does not falter"?

In what book does a "pigeon-hearted" man prefer pardoning prisoners to executing them, saying that it rested him to think of excuses for saving "some poor fellow's life"?

In what book is there a president who has a terrible time finding capable generals to fight a war?

What book tells about a man who became president by the votes of only the Northern states?

Lion, the Witch and the Wardrobe, The
Lewis, C. S.

In what book is there a witch who rules a country that is always cold and wintery?

In what book were some children referred to as the Sons of Adam and Daughters of Eve?

In what book did some stone statues come to life after a lion sacrificed himself?

In what book does a brother succumb to the charms of a woman with some sweet candy called "Turkish Delight"?

In what book is there a lion named Aslan?

Little House in the Big Woods
Wilder, Laura Ingalls

In which book do two girls use a pig's bladder as a balloon?

In what book does a family put hot potatoes in their pockets to keep their fingers warm?

In what book are a girl's favorite days the ones when her mother bakes and when her father plays the fiddle?

In which book are the children told a story about grandpa and the black panther?

In which book did someone collect so many pebbles that they tore out the pocket of her best dress?

Little Man, The
Kastner, Eric

In what book does the wind blow the main character off the Empire State Building?

In what book is a tiny boy kidnapped so he can be sold to a wealthy art collector?

In what book does the hero learn to read by running up and down a ladder to see the words in the book?

In what book is there a man named Maxie Pickelsteiner?

In what book does the hero learn to be a magician's assistant by climbing all over a department store mannequin?

Little Men
Alcott, Louisa May

In what book do Jo and her husband, Professor Bhaer, run a school for boys?

In what book does a family take in a couple of homeless boys? One has been a street musician; the other fought for his survival.

In what book is Dan told to leave school because he's taught the other boys to drink, swear, smoke, and play poker?

In what book do Nan and Rob get lost while picking huckleberries?

In what book is Nat accused of stealing Tommy's money? Dan takes the blame, even though Jack is the culprit.

Little Prince, The
Saint-Exupery, Antoine De

In what book does a boy draw a picture of a boa constrictor digesting an elephant?

In what book does a boy love his flower?

In what book does the main character meet a lot of strange grown-ups, such as the businessman who counts all the stars he thinks he owns?

In what book does a pilot meet a boy who insists he is a prince from asteroid B-612?

In what book are some baobob trees a real danger to an asteroid?

Little Women
Alcott, Louisa May

In what book does Jo still like to climb trees and ride horses although she is old enough to "act like a lady"?

In what book does Amy fall in love with Laurie?

In what book does Beth's sister write her a poem telling her how much she will be missed when she dies?

In what book is a girl's father taken ill during the Civil War? She sells her hair for $25 to help her mother travel to be with him.

In what book do four lively sisters help their mother cope while their father is away at the Civil War?

Lone Hunt, The
Steele, William O.

In what book does Yancy lose most of his ammunition when climbing a mountain?

In what book does Pleasant do the outdoor work on the farm while the boy has to help in the house?

What book is about the last buffalo hunt in Tennessee?

In which book does Yancy finally kill his buffalo, but also loses his dog, Blue?

In what book does a boy decide to go hunting for a buffalo by himself?

Luck of Pokey Bloom, The
Conford, Ellen

In which book do the "Girls Against Garbage" plan to clean up a vacant lot, but then get into a litter fight with the boys?

In which book was a girl told that concentrating on winning would make her win the prize?

In which book does a woman buy greeting cards after the salesperson tells her that "they're cheap enough for a cheapskate"?

In which book does Charlotte win a transistor radio in a cake contest?

In what book does a girl love entering all sorts of sweepstakes contests?

M. C. Higgins the Great
Hamilton, Virginia

In what book does the hero dream that his mother will become a country music star?

In what book does the main character spend hours sitting on top of a forty-foot pole outside his house?

In what book is a coal slag heap moving down the mountain?

In what book does a young black boy trap and hunt rabbits to help feed his family when his father isn't working?

In what book is there a character named Mayo Cornelius?

Magic Hat of Mortimer Wintergreen, The
LeVoy, Myron

In what book is there a mean woman who holds up signs with numbers for the chores the children are to do or the punishments they will get?

In what book do some bandits get trapped by armfuls of soft taffy when they reach into a hat for hidden gold?

In what book does Aunt Vootch make Joshua and Amy live in a pigpen?

In what book do a magician and some children arrive in New York by balloon, which later is used to take their evil aunt and the Slickers away?

In what book do Amy and Josh live with Aunt Vootch, the meanest woman in South Dakota?

Maniac Magee
Spinelli, Jerry

Who won a year's worth of pizzas by untying the famous cobble's knot?

In what book does a homeless boy sleep in the zoo with the deer and the buffalo?

In what book did Amanda decide to change a bully's name from Mars Bar to Snickers?

In what book did Jeffrey find homes and acceptance with the black kids from the East End and also the white kids from the West End?

In what book did Grayson tell about the time he struck out Willie Mays?

Mariah Delaney Lending Library Disaster, The
Greenwald, Sheila

In what book does a girl decide to compete with the Public Library?

In what book does a girl decide to start loaning out her own books?

In what book are a girl's parents worried about all her wheeling and dealing?

In what book does a girl loan out all her mother's cookbooks?

In what book do the friends forget to return all the items they've borrowed?

Mary Poppins
Travers, P. L.

In what book do Jane and Michael spend the day with their nurse-maid inside a sidewalk chalk drawing?

In which book does the main character have an umbrella with a parrot handle?

In what book do Jane and Michael find themselves so full of laughing gas that they float in the air?

Who comes to take care of Jane, Michael, and the twins?

In what book does a nursemaid tell about how the respectable red cow wound up jumping over the moon?

Matchlock Gun, The
Edmonds, Walter

In which book is Edward told to shoot *only* if his mother calls him by the name Ateoord?

In what book does a little New York Dutch boy save his family from the Indians by firing off his family's old Spanish gun?

In what book is a small New York Dutch boy left alone with his mother and baby sister during the French and Indian War?

In what book does a boy's little sister call a gun "Bergen Op Zoom"?

In what book is a ten-year-old left to help his mother fight Indians?

Me and Caleb
Meyers, Franklyn

In what book is there a dog named Petunia?

In what book do two brothers find a starving mother dog and her dead pups under the house?

In which book do the boys paint doorknobs with bacon grease?

In what book does Bud hide the goat that is to be his father's Christmas present in a closet, where it almost eats his father's new suit?

In what book does a boy go hand fishing for eels, and get a water moccasin wrapped around his arm instead?

Meet Samantha
Adler, Susan

In which book does Uncle Gard give our heroine a ride in one of the first automobiles in town?

In what book does a little girl live with her grandmother who is called "Grandmary"?

In which book does Jessie leave her job without any explanation to the little girl who loves her?

In which book do two little girls go out at night to find out why Jessie has left her job as a seamstress?

In which book does nine-year-old Nellie work as a maid, which she thinks is much better than her former job in a factory?

Megan's Island
Roberts, Willo Davis

In what book does a girl begin to wonder why her mother changes jobs and towns so often?

In what book is a girl upset because she can't tell her best friend where she's moved to?

In what book is a girl scared when she finds out that a strange man is pretending to be the uncle of two red-headed kids?

In what book does a girl find a birth certificate for a girl named Margaret Anne and suddenly realizes that it must be her own certificate, even though it's not her name?

In what book do some children hide in their island tree house when they find a stranger looking for them?

Miracles on Maple Hill
Sorensen, Virginia

In what book do Marly and Joe help save a family of foxes from bounty hunters?

In what book is the truant officer known as "Annie-get-your-gun"?

In what book does the book begin and end during the sugaring-off season?

In what book do the children help with making maple sugar after Mr. Chris gets sick?

In what book is Marly's father recovering from the ordeal of having been a prisoner of war?

Miss Hickory
Bailey, Carolyn

In what book does a doll sew her own clothes out of leaves?

In what book does a doll spend the winter in a nest?

Who was the little lady who lived in a corncob house?

What's the name of the doll whose head is made from a nut? The answer is the name of the book.

In what book does a cow save a doll from freezing?

Miss Pickerell Goes to Mars
MacGregor, Ellen

What lady finds a strange contraption about to leave Earth from her pasture?

In what book does a woman find herself on a spaceship by mistake?

In what book does a person find herself cured of her dizziness after a space trip?

In what book does a sick cow lead to a space adventure?

In what book does a magnetic hammer ruin the calibration of some electronic instruments?

Missing May
Rylant, Cynthia

In what book does an orphan girl go to live with some old people in a rusty antiquated trailer?

In what book does a little girl feel right at home when she sees her new house has lots of whirligigs and chocolate milk?

In what book is there a weird boy who collects pictures from cereal boxes, tin cans, old circulars, and anything else he can find?

In what book does Summer find peace in the swoop of an owl's wings?

In what book do some characters set out to visit a Small Medium At Large, who is also known as the Bat Lady?

Misty of Chincoteague
Henry, Marguerite

What book is about an island on which wild ponies have lived since the days of the Spanish sailing ships?

In what book is a colt described as looking as if he has come out of the sea?

In what book do Maureen and Paul earn $100 for Pony Penning Day?

What book is about the yearly roundup of the wild ponies of Assateague Island?

In what book is there a horse considered to be uncatchable?

Molly's Pilgrim
Cohen, Barbara

In which book do a group of third-grade girls laugh at a little girl with imperfect English and old country clothes?

In which book does a Jewish girl long to return to her home in Russia where she won't be teased, but knows she can't because the Cossacks are causing harm to the Jewish people?

In which book does a third-grade class learn that "it takes all kinds of pilgrims to make a Thanksgiving"?

In which book is a third-grade girl reluctant to have her mother meet her teacher, because her mother cannot speak English and she feels ashamed?

In which book does a third-grade girl hide a beautiful clothespin doll her mother made because it doesn't look like the dolls the other boys and girls have made?

Mouse and the Motorcycle, The
Cleary, Beverly

In which book does a small animal have to struggle to keep from being sucked into the vacuum cleaner?

In which book does a mouse get caught in a pillowcase and dumped in the hamper?

In which book does a small animal find and bring an aspirin to his sick friend, Keith?

In which book is a small animal trapped in a metal wastebasket?

In which book does the noise "pb pb bb" cause a motorcycle to run?

Mr. Popper's Penguins
Atwater, Richard

In what book do some people toboggan on the ice inside their own house?

In what book does a family flood their basement and let it freeze to make living quarters for their pet animals?

In what book does a man want to have air holes put in his refrigerator door?

In which book do some animals climb up and down all the ladders, and jump into all the berths on a sleeping car?

In what book does Admiral Drake send a bird from the South Pole to an unemployed house painter?

Mrs. Frisby and the Rats of NIMH
O'Brien, Robert

In what book does Jeremy the crow fly off with two mice clinging to his beak?

In what book do some animals use their ability to read in order to escape their cages?

In what book does Nicodemus help create a city complete with electricity?

What is the title of the book about a laboratory called the National Institute of Mental Health?

In what book does a widowed mouse seek help from some wise rats?

Mrs. Piggle Wiggle
MacDonald, Betty

Who cures all problem children like the "never-want-to-go-to-Bedders"?

In what book is there a rude parrot that cures "answer-backers"?

Who lives in a house that is built upside down?

What book is about a woman who works to cure children's bad habits? She has a selfishness kit made up of lots of padlocks and labels.

Who suggested planting radishes on a little girl who didn't want to take baths?

My Daniel
Conrad, Pam

In what book does Ellie wonder why her grandmother wants to take her on a secret mission to the Natural History Museum?

In what book does Ellie keep the museum guard away while her grandmother climbs up on the dinosaur skeleton?

In what book does a boy find giant dinosaur bones?

In what book does a wooden-legged villain ride a camel in Nebraska?

In what book is a boy killed in a lightning storm?

My Side of the Mountain
George, Jean

In what book does Sam train a falcon to hunt for him?

In what book is there a raccoon named "Jessie Coon James"?

In what book does Sam wear rabbit skins under his clothes?

What book has a recipe for frog soup served in a turtle shell?

In what book does a boy live by himself in a hollow tree and eat what the animals find safe?

Not Just Anybody Family, The
Byars, Betsy

In what book does a grandfather collect beer cans in order to raise money for the family?

In what book did Junior break his legs by falling off a barn roof with cloth wings tied to his arms?

In what book does a boy break into jail to rescue his grandfather?

In what book does Junior attempt to fly off the barn with his homemade wings?

In what book does Pap drop 2,147 beer cans from his truck in the center of town?

Number the Stars
Lowry, Lois

In what book does a girl discover that it is really easier to be brave if one doesn't know everything that is going on?

In what book does Annamarie smuggle a handkerchief to her uncle, one that has a powerful scent to confuse the search dogs?

In what book do the people pretend to be gathering for Aunt Birte's funeral, though they are really planning to escape?

In what book does Annamarie's father convince the soldiers that Ellen is his daughter, even though she has dark hair?

What book takes place in Denmark during the World War II German occupation?

Old Yeller
Gipson, Fred

In what book does a dog get hurt by a wild pig?

In what book does a boy find his hound dog is also a good hog dog?

In what book does a boy have to shoot his dog after it's been attacked by a killer wolf?

What book is about a family living in Texas on Birdsong Creek?

In what book is a thieving hound adopted by Little Arliss?

On My Honor
Bauer, Marion

In what book does a boy decide not to tell anyone about the drowning of his best friend?

In what book does a boy feel guilty because Tony's accident happened after Joel broke his promise to his father?

In what book does a boy bet another about swimming out to a sandbar?

In what book does Joel find himself usually doing the things his friend wants to do, rather than the things he wants to do himself?

In what book does the title refer to the promises Joel makes to his father?

On to Oregon
Morrow, Honore

In what book do some freezing children find hot springs?

In what book does a boy decide not to stay at Fort Hall with the soldiers?

In what book do some children meet a half-Spanish girl who is running away from her father?

In what book is a family saved from the Sioux by Kit Carson?

In what book does a boy named John take care of his family by himself?

Over Sea, under Stone
Cooper, Susan

In which book does Uncle Merry Lyon represent Merlin?

In which book does the mysterious Mr. Withers prove to be one of the forces of evil?

In what book does Uncle Merry Lyon represent the forces of good?

In what book do some children find the Holy Grail?

In what book do Jane, Simon and Barney find an old map in an attic?

Owls in the Family
Mowat, Farley

What book tells the adventures of Wol and Weeps, two birds from Saskatchewan?

In what book does Wol deposit a skunk at the family dinner table?

In what book is there a bird who never learns to fly because he is always so frightened?

In what book does a boy named Billy find a bird in an oil barrel?

In what book do two boys bring a rattlesnake to the parade in order to win the prize for the most unusual pet?

Paddle-to-the-Sea
Holling, Holling C.

In which book is a canoe saved just in time from being split by a saw in a sawmill?

In which book does a hand-carved canoe begin a long trip to the sea from the top of a snow-covered hill?

In which book does a miniature canoe plunge over Niagara Falls into the rapids of the Niagara River?

In which book does a canoe witness a forest fire and a shipwreck, while it also survives storms and wild currents on its trip to the sea?

In which book does a young boy carve the figure of an Indian in a canoe and send him off on a long journey?

Paul Bunyan Swings His Axe
McCormick, Dell

In which book is a baby ox found half buried under blue snow?

In what book does a man run so fast that he outraces the buck-shot he's fired at a bear—and gets the buckshot in his own seat instead?

In what book does a man named Johnnie Inkslinger use up a whole barrel of ink every two days?

In what book is there a sidehill goat with short legs on one side so it doesn't fall off a mountain, and sundodger birds that lay square eggs so they won't roll?

What book tells about such characters as Hot Biscuit Slim, Ole the Big Swede, Brimstone Bill, and Cream Puff Fatty?

Peel the Extraordinary Elephant
Joyce, Susan

Who found out he was unique when an owl told him that learning was what made him extraordinary?

Who gets his name from a camel named Camille? The answer is the title of this book.

Who learned how to swim from a fish?

Who learned to dance from an ant?

In what book is the main character wakened from a nap by a slurping sound of a creature with "a bump on its back and brown shaggy hair"?

Peter Pan
Barrie, J. M.

In what book do the children fly following the directions "second star to the right and straight on till morning"?

In what book is Wendy's life saved by the kiss she wears around her neck?

In what book does Tink drink the poisoned medicine meant for someone else?

In what book is there an evil pirate named Captain Hook?

In which book do the children fly away to Never Never Land?

Peter Potts
Hicks, Clifford

In which book do the kids blow the dirt from the vacuum cleaner all over the living room?

In which book does the champion speller write a message on the water tower in town—and every word he writes is misspelled?

In which book does a boy ride his brakeless soapbox racer down the main street until he hits a fire hydrant?

In which book does a boy use Ostermeyer's barn for the "World's Biggest Wedding Reception"?

In which book do all Joey's efforts to help Pete pull his loose tooth backfire? He ends up being hit by a door, a barbeque, and fence boards.

Phantom Tollboth, The
Juster, Norton

In what book does a boy travel through "The Valley of Sound," "Dictionopolis," and "Digitopolis"?

In what book do we find a watchdog with the body of a loudly ticking alarm clock?

In what book does a boy get hungrier the more he eats of Subtraction Stew?

In what book does Milo meet the Dodecahedron, a character with twelve faces?

In what book is there a "Castle in the Air"?

Philip Hall Likes Me I Reckon, Maybe
Greene, Bette

In what book does a girl deliberately do less than her best so a boy can be tops in the class?

In what book does Beth capture the turkey thieves?

In what book do the Pretty Pennies picket a cheating storekeeper?

In what book do the girls' embroidered club T-shirts shrink so much in the wash that they can't be worn?

In what book does Beth rescue a boy with a hurt foot?

Pinballs, The
Byars, Betsy

What book is about Carlie who's been beaten by her stepfather?

In what book does Harvey say that his legs were broken in a football game instead of telling about being run over by his father?

In what book was one of the main characters left in front of a farmhouse and raised by two elderly twins?

In what book is a puppy smuggled into a hospital as a birthday present so a boy will have something to love?

In what book does Harvey make a list of "Bad Things That Have Happened to Me" and "Gifts I Got That I Didn't Want"?

Pinch
Callen, Larry

In what book is the main character always getting beat in trades by a very tricky skinflint?

In what book does the hero trade a quarter for a frog, a frog for two chickens, and the chickens for a pig—and then almost trades the pig for a dying mule?

Who owns the best hunting pig in Four Corners?

In what book does Billy Sweet coat a pig with soot and boot polish?

In what book does a boy round up some pigs for John Barrow, and then is cheated out of his money?

Pippi Longstocking
Lindgren, Astrid

In which book does a girl beat Mighty Adolf, the circus strongman, and wins $100?

Who believed that her father was a cannibal king and lived in the Villa Villekulla?

In what book does a nine-year-old girl easily pick up big bullies?

What little girl lives alone with a horse and a monkey?

What child rescues two little boys from a fire in the tallest building in town—which is three stories high?

Pushcart War, The
Merrill, Jean

In what book does the girl's family move to twenty-nine houses in twenty-eight years?

In what book is *Pilgrim's Progress* the favorite book of a school teacher father?

What book is about a pea shooter campaign?

In what book does General Anna attack the trucks by hand?

In what book do the children form a "Frank-the-Flower" club?

Quest for a Maid
Hendry, Frances Mary

In what book is nine-year-old Meg betrothed to six-year-old Davie because she is the only one who can understand his speech?

In what book does Meg try to save her sister Inge from being tried for witchcraft? Her testimony only makes things worse.

In what book does a girl save the life of the Norwegian princess who is to become Queen of the Scots?

In what book does a boy with speech problems due to a harelip learn to read and write several languages.

In what book does Peem run away from the lord who plans to cut off his foot as a punishment? He's saved because the lord doesn't know his name.

Rabbit Hill
Lawson, Robert

In what book does little Georgie jump eighteen feet over Deadman's Brook?

In which book does little Georgie's father make him memorize the neighborhood dogs?

In what book is little Georgie sent to fetch Uncle Analdas?

In what book do the animals wonder if the new people will be the kind who plant or the kind who use poison and guns?

In what book was a statue of St. Francis given to the animals as a gift?

Ramona and Her Father
Cleary, Beverly

In what book does a girl ask for "one happy family" for Christmas instead of a cuckoo clock?

In what book does a girl make a crown out of burrs, only to find they all stick in her hair?

In what book does a girl put signs all over the house to help her father quit smoking?

In what book does someone have to wear her old pajamas as part of her sheep costume?

In what book does the Christmas pageant have three wise *persons* instead of three wise *men*?

Ramona Forever
Cleary, Beverly

In what book is the expected baby called Algie?

In what book does the heroine discover she will no longer be the baby in the family?

In what book does Uncle Hobart plan the entire wedding and do all the shopping?

In what book does Uncle Hobart bring Howie a camel seat from Saudi Arabia?

In what book does Aunt Beatrice teach third grade?

Ramona Quimby, Age 8
Cleary, Beverly

In what book is the heroine bored by having to stay with Willa Jean Kemp?

In what book is there a teacher named Mrs. Whaley—spelled like a "whale with a Y"?

In which book is the main character called "Bigfoot" and "Egghead" by her friend "Yard Ape"?

In what book does the heroine crack a raw egg on her head?

In which book does a girl get her friends to wear cat masks and meow, while she gives her book report?

Rascal
North, Sterling

In what book does a boy have a pet raccoon who rides in his bicycle basket?

In what book does a pet raccoon have to be locked up after he raids the neighborhood for sweet corn?

In what book does a St. Bernard dig a baby animal out of a tree stump?

In what book does Sterling build a canoe in the living room?

In what book does a boy have pet skunks, woodchucks, and cats, as well as a pet raccoon and a crow?

Rascals from Haskells Gym, The
Bonham, Frank

In which book is Sissy's father fixing up an old hotel?

In what book is an old church used as a gym?

In which book does Sissy drip ink on Lori's sleeve so the twins can be told apart during the match?

What book is about two rival gymnastics teams?

In which book is Sissy called "the iron butterfly" by the local sports reporters?

Redwall
Jacques, Brian

In what book does Cluny the Scourge plot to take over the abbey in Mossflower Wood?

In what book does Matthias discover that his name is an anagram for "I am that is"?

In what book does a mouse convert the enemy sparrows into becoming part of his invading army?

In what book does the snake Asmodeus guard the sword that once belonged to Martin the Warrior?

In what book will you meet good and evil characters such as Silent Sam, Basil Stag Hare, Warbeak, Chicken Hound, and Dark Claw?

Reluctant Dragon, The
Grahame, Kenneth

In which book is the title character "quite lazy when it comes to being a fearsome beast"?

In which book does the title character refuse to fight St. George?

In which book do a boy and his father discover a fearsome creature on the downs?

In which book does the boy concoct a clever plan to keep the title character from becoming hurt in a fight?

In which book does an entire village befriend a mild-mannered dragon?

Rifles for Watie
Keith, Harold

In what book does Jefferson Davis Bussey join the Union army after his family is attacked by Missouri bushwhackers?

In what book are the civilized Cherokee Indians supporters of the Confederate army?

In what book does a Union scout find himself a member of the Rebel army?

In what book do the Cherokee Indians take the South's side in the Civil War?

In what book does Jeff, a Union soldier, fall in love with Lucy, a rebel Cherokee?

Rikki Tikki Tavi
Kipling, Rudyard

Which book is about Teddy and his pet mongoose?

In what book is Nagaina just as wicked as Nag?

In which book is there an evil character named Nag?

In which book does a mongoose fight some cobras?

In which book are there some characters named Nag, Darzee, Karait, and Chuchundra?

Roll of Thunder, Hear My Cry
Taylor, Mildred

In what book is the Logan family resented only because they are black?

In what book do the black children have to dodge a school bus full of white children every day?

In what book do the black children have to use the worn-out textbooks discarded from the white schools?

In what book does a teacher lose her job when the black families boycott a white-owned store?

In what book do the black children have to walk to school, while the white children ride the school bus?

Russell Sprouts
Hurwitz, Johanna

In which book does a six-year-old boy not want to "hand-me-up" his new, too large, red rain slicker to the boy upstairs?

In which book does a six-year-old boy make up his own, imaginary bad word to use when he is angry?

In which book does a six-year-old boy give his parents a report card with low grades for television, cookies, presents, bedtime and yelling?

In which book does a six-year-old boy dress up as a daddy for Halloween?

In which book does a six-year-old boy become lost in a movie theater complex and end up watching a scary movie about a fire?

Sarah Plain and Tall
MacLachlan, Patricia

In what book did Caleb wish he could remember his mother, who died the day after he was born?

In what book do Anna and Caleb hope the woman from Maine will become their stepmother?

In what book does a woman leave her seaside home in Maine for a new life on the Great Plains?

In what book does a woman answer an ad for a mail-order wife?

In what book does a woman love the colors of the sea, blue and gray and green?

Save Queen of Sheba
Moeri, Louise

In what book does a boy have to decide whether to stay in the shelter of a cave, or try to set out and find the trail of the other wagons?

In what book does a boy rescue his lost sister from an Indian woman?

In what book is a boy nearly scalped during a Sioux Indian raid?

In what book does a boy find that he and his sister are the only survivors of an Indian attack on their wagon train?

In what book is a boy tempted to stop looking for his little sister?

Scrub Fire
De Roo, Anne

In what book does a fire separate Michelle and her little brother from their aunt and uncle?

In what book do three children survive on their own after a terrible forest fire?

In what book does Michelle dread the camping trip with her uncle and aunt?

In what book does Michelle find out her little brothers actually know a lot about how to survive in the Australian bush?

In what book do the children eat fern roots for food?

Sea Pup
Binns, Archie

In what book does Clint adopt a baby seal after its mother has been shot?

In what book do Clint and his family send a troublemaking animal up to Alaska—only to have him arrive back home a week later?

In what book does a boy write a research paper on geoducks?

In what book does an animal get in trouble for milking cows?

In what book does a pet named Buster always know when it is time for Clint to come home?

Searching for Shona
Anderson, Margaret

In what book does rich Marjorie find happiness taking care of a little orphan named Anna?

In what book do two girls change places during a World War II evacuation?

In what book does Marjorie find Anna hiding in an empty house with lots of toys?

In what book does Marjorie discover the secret of another girl's past?

In what book is a girl supposed to go to Canada to be safe from the German bombings?

Secret Friend, A
Sachs, Marilyn

In what book does Jessica think that her best friend is fun and exciting, but also knows that she likes to be mean?

In what book does Jessica's best friend decide to ignore her and instead becomes best friends with Barbara?

In what book are the notes a girl gets in school the first secret she's ever kept from her mom?

In what book does a girl talk to everyone in her class trying to find out who's writing notes to her?

In what book does Sister Helen say that friends pick each other, should have common interests, and support and help each other when needed?

Secret Garden, The
Burnett, Frances H.

In what book are two children kept in an old house where the boy does not want the girl ever to see him?

In what book does a curious robin help a girl find an old key?

In what book is there a ten-year-old boy who believes he will have crooked legs when he grows up?

In what book does Dickon teach Colin that the best magic is in taking care of an old garden?

In what book is a there a boy nicknamed "The Young Rajah" and a girl nicknamed "Mistress Mary Quite Contrary"?

Secret Life of Dilly McBean, The
Haas, Dorothy

In what book is a boy left an orphan to be brought up by a bank and trust company?

In what book does a boy name his dog Contrary because he does exactly the opposite of whatever he's told?

In what book is a boy kidnapped by Dr. Keenwit, owner of the Great Harmonizer Computer?

In what book does a famous scientist, Dr. McEvoy, offer to help develop a boy's talent?

In what book is a boy in danger of being kidnapped because of a special talent he inherited?

Secret of The Andes
Clark, Ann Nolan

In what book does Cusi live with Chuto, the old Inca llama herder?

In what book is there a boy who wears golden plugs in his ears?

In what book does a boy learn how to train his pet llama to carry burdens?

In what book does an Indian boy live in a hidden valley with only an old herder to keep him and his llamas company?

Which book is supposed to be about an Inca boy living in modern times?

Shiloh
Naylor, Phyllis

In what book does a boy promise to work for a man he dislikes—and keeps his promise even after the man states he won't keep his side of the bargain?

In what book does Marty find a dog who won't come when he's called, although he answers to a whistle?

In what book does a boy spend hours collecting bottles and cans so he won't have to return a dog to his abusive owner?

In what book does Marty hide some of his own food each day so he can feed a dog he's keeping secret from his family?

In what book does a German shepherd brutally attack a dog who's being hidden in a remote hillside pen?

Shoeshine Girl
Bulla, Clyde

In which book does Sarah Ida talk her new friend into loaning her money?

In what book is Sarah Ida given the keys to a business?

In what book does Sarah shine shoes to earn money?

In what book is Sarah Ida sent away to live with Aunt Claudia because her best friend is a shoplifter?

In what book does a girl have to earn her own pocket money?

Sign of The Beaver, The
Speare, Elizabeth

In what book does a stranger steal Matt's gun—his only weapon and means of getting game?

In what book is Matt left alone in the new cabin while his father goes back for his mother and the new baby?

In what book does the Indian grandfather make a treaty with Matt? He will bring Matt food if Matt will teach Attean how to read.

In what book does Attean show Matt how to make fish hooks and a snare to catch small game?

In what book does reading the story of Robinson Crusoe bring a white boy and an Indian boy closer to understanding one another?

Sixth Grade Can Really Kill You
De Clements, Barthe

In what book does Helen know she needs help with her reading, but her mother does not agree?

In what book does Helen fight being sent to special education because she thinks her friends will tease her?

In what book does Helen play practical jokes in school?

In what book does a girl shoot off firecrackers in school and in camp?

In what book does Helen feel she's dumb because of her reading problems, even though she is smart in other things?

Slave Dancer, The
Fox, Paula

In what book do Jessie Bollier and Ras escape a ship carrying illegal cargo?

In what book are the black people dropped into the sea when an American ship comes too close?

In what book is Jessie Bollier imprisoned on a ship because he can play a fife?

In what book does a ship's cargo consist of ninety-eight men, women, and children?

In what book was the first mate dropped overboard because he killed a black man who was worth good money?

Smallest Monster in the World, The
MacKellar, William

In what book is there a Kelpie named Mr. Peebles?

What book is about a very shy plesiosaur named Maggie?

In what book does his ninth birthday destroy a boy's ability to see his friend Mr. Peebles?

In what book does a five-foot-long plesiosaur show up at three o'clock on Saturday afternoon?

In what book do the townspeople decide they don't want to have a Loch Ness–type monster, after the tourists and TV people mess up the town?

Smoke
Corbin, William

In what book does Chris's stepfather ban all dogs from his sheep ranch?

In what book does Chris run away with a dog so he won't have to give him up?

In what book does Chris realize that his stepfather deserves respect and is really on his side?

In what book does Chris rescue a starving dog—and finds out that the dog belongs to an old man who was injured in an automobile accident?

In what book is Chris afraid that his stepfather will shoot the dog he is hiding?

Smoky the Cow Horse
James, Will

What book tells the story of a wild horse and a cowboy named Clint?

In what book does Clint find his former bucking horse mistreated and hitched to a vegetable wagon? Clint nurses him back to health.

What book is supposed to be a true story about a cow pony?

In what book does a cow pony turn into a killer bronc?

In what book is a bucking horse promoted for competitions as "The Cougar"?

Snow Treasure
McSwigan, Marie

In which book is Peter's Uncle Victor asked to help smuggle a German soldier to America?

In what book do some Norwegian children rescue gold bars from the Nazis?

In what book does the town doctor paint red spots on all the children so they don't have to go to school?

In which book do the children hide gold bricks on their sled?

In which book do the Germans land in Norway by parachute and submarine?

Sounder
Armstrong, William

In what book does a mother feed her family by selling walnuts?

In what book does a hound dog die soon after his master does?

In what book does a boy use old newspapers to practice his reading?

In what book is the father sent to prison for stealing a ham?

In what book does a boy follow chain gangs across the South as he looks for his father?

Soup and Me
Peck, Robert

In what book does Janice Riker throw all the boy's clothes in Putt's Pond?

In what book do the boys use a silver hot water tank as the body of a soapbox racer?

In what book do two boys crash their pumpkin into the Baptist church?

In what book does a boy's best friend rub the Pink Awful gum into his hair?

In which book do some boys try to ring the church bell as a Christmas present for their teacher?

Stone Fox
Gardiner, John

In what book did the man from the state of Wyoming tell little Willy he would take the farm away unless he paid $500?

In what book does a dog die only ten feet from the finish line?

In what book did a boy enter the dogsled races because he needed money for the farm?

In what book does an Indian let a boy win a race by walking to the finish line?

In what book is an Indian using the money he wins to buy back the lands that used to belong to the Shoshone?

Story of Dr. Doolittle, The
Lofting, Hugh

In what book does a doctor have so many animal patients that he makes special doors for all the different kinds?

In what book did some animals and a doctor save a little boy who had been captured by pirates?

In what book is there a two-headed animal that claimed to be descended from the last of the unicorns?

In what book do the monkeys capture a pushmi-pullyu, so that the man who cured them can make some money in the Land of the White Man?

In what book were some favorite pets named Dab Dab, Jip, Gub Gub, Polynesia, and Too Too?

Story of King Arthur and His Knights, The
Pyle, Howard

In what book does a boy turn out to be the only one who can gain the sword that makes him King of England?

In what book do men search for a cup that Jesus is said to have used at the Last Supper?

In what book did the Lady in the Lake present a sword called Excalibur to the main character?

In what book does a king's son work in a kitchen for a year because he's promised his mother that he will not fight?

In what book is a child hidden away by a wizard in order to save his life?

Stout-Hearted Seven, The
Frazier, Neta

In which book do the Sager children witness an Indian massacre?

In which book does the father promise that, after the family gets to Oregon, he will never ask his wife to move again?

In which book is an orphaned family looked after by a German doctor?

In what book are some children left to travel alone after their mother dies?

In what book is a family of orphaned children taken in by Dr. and Mrs. Whitman?

Strawberry Girl
Lenski, Lois

In what book does the lazy Slater family resent the Boyer family because they are hard workers?

In what book do the Slaters and Boyers have a feud going over hogs, cows, fences and just about everything else?

In what book does Birdie try to make friends with her hateful neighbors?

In what book does a family burn down the school when they attempt to burn out another family?

What book tells about the lives of people called "Florida Crackers"?

Stuart Little
White, E. B.

In which book does the new baby in the family "look very much like a mouse in every way"?

In which book does a mouse sail a schooner in a race across a pond in Central Park?

In which book does a mouse, trapped in a garbage truck, get dumped on a garbage scow being towed out to sea?

In which book does a mouse substitute for a teacher at Public School No. 7 who has fallen ill?

In which book does a mouse search for a lost bird by traveling in a miniature car that can become invisible?

Summer of the Monkeys
Rawls, Wilson

In which book do a boy and his hound dog discover some circus animals in the trees near his home?

In which book does a boy's sister need an operation for a twisted leg? His family can't afford to pay for it.

In which book does a boy set out to earn the reward money posted for anyone who captures the animals that escaped from a circus train?

In which book do a boy, his dog, and some monkeys discover a still in the woods by the river bottoms? They become tipsy and very ill from drinking its contents.

In which book does a boy decide to give his reward money to his parents to pay for his sister's badly needed operation instead of using it to buy the horse he wants for himself?

Summer of the Swans
Byars, Betsy

In what book does Sara discover she's been mistaken about Joe Melby—that he's not a thief after all?

In what book does Sara spend hours looking for her retarded brother who is lost?

In which book is retarded Charlie fascinated by watching the large white birds on the lake?

In which book does Sara feel that she's not pretty, not a good dancer, not anything? Her sister says she's a good dishwasher.

In which book does Charlie decide to look for some birds during the night?

Superfudge
Blume, Judy

In what book does Peter get a little sister named Tootsie?

In what book does a kindergarten child talk the visiting author into drawing a picture of the school principal?

In what book is Peter's little brother jealous of the new baby, Tootsie?

In what book is a baby covered with trading stamps?

In what book does a boy have a pet myna bird named Uncle Feather?

Swiss Family Robinson, The
Wyss, J. R.

In what book does a family make a boat out of old wooden casks, so they can leave a ship and get ashore?

In what book does a family build a tree house they call Falconhurst?

In what book does a family, marooned on an island, discover Jenny who has also been marooned for three years?

In what book does a family kill a boa constrictor after watching him swallow their donkey?

In what book does a family have to choose between returning to England or staying on their island of New Switzerland?

Switcharound
Lowry, Lois

In what book does J.P. finally prove to his dad that he knows computers well enough to straighten out the financial records in the store?

In what book do Caroline and J.P. find themselves spending a whole summer in Iowa with their divorced father?

In what book does J.P. plan to take revenge on his dad by making the Little League team lose the big game?

In what book does Caroline, who hates babies, have to babysit her twin half-sisters, Holly and Ivy?

In what book does Caroline take revenge on her dad by mixing up the twins' colors so they can't tell which twin is which?

Tales of a Fourth Grade Nothing
Blume, Judy

In what book does Fudge try to be a bird by jumping off the monkey bars?

In what book is there a contest to win a turtle by guessing the number of jelly beans in a jar?

In what book does Peter's little brother make commercials for television ?

In what book does Fudge swallow a turtle?

In what book did a little boy get tired of the Juice-O his father advertises?

Tales of Olga Da Polga, The
Bond, Michael

In what book does a guinea pig tell fantastic tales to her friends?

In what book is there a guinea pig who wants to "go places"?

In what book does a guinea pig leave a pet shop to go with "the sawdust people"?

In what book does a guinea pig tell her friends fantastic tales?

In what book does a greedy animal get a rosette for being the fattest animal in the show?

Tales of Uncle Remus, The
Lester, Julius

In what book does a turtle family hide behind trees in order to win a race?

In what book is a tar baby made and used to trap an animal?

In what book is Brer Wolf tricked into believing his cow has gone underground?

In what book does a rabbit watch a man build a trap for him and tricks a wolf into going inside the trap instead?

In what book do Brer Rabbit and Brer Fox constantly try to get the best of one another?

Ten Kids, No Pets
Martin, Ann

In what book is Ira afraid that he won't be liked because he has nine brothers and sisters, all with weird names?

In what book does Mrs. Rosso have systems for everything, including packing lunches, folding laundry, how kids should sit in the car, and naming new babies?

In what book does Candy discover a secret room?

In what book does a city family move to a farm with absolutely no animals?

In what book do the children name the turkey that is to be used for Thanksgiving dinner—and are then unwilling to let him be killed?

There's a Boy in the Girl's Bathroom
Sachar, Louis

In what book is Bradley described as looking like a good spitter?

In what book is a boy confused when Jeff Fishkin actually wants to be his friend?

In what book does the school counselor keep saying that all she can do is to help kids think for themselves?

In what book do two boys get black eyes from Melinda, but blame each other rather than letting others know that they came from a girl?

In what book does a fifth-grade boy get invited to his very first birthday party?

Thimble Summer
Enright, Elizabeth

In what book does Garnet find a lucky object?

In what book does a farm family take in Eric Swanstrom, an orphan boy who is surviving on his own?

In what book does Garnet's prize hog Timmy win a blue ribbon?

In what book do Garnet and Citronella get locked in the public library?

In what book do two little girls get stranded at the top of a ferris wheel?

Thirteen Ways to Sink a Sub
Gilson, Jamie

In what book are the kids giving a report on China?

In what book is the star character a lady named Svetlana Ivanovitch?

In what book do the students flood their classroom?

In what book does the class appreciate Ms. Ivanovitch who can throw snowballs and paper airplanes and knows how to folk dance?

In what book do the girls have a bet with the boys, and the losers have to get balls out from the spit pit?

Three Knocks on the Wall
Lampman, Evelyn Sibley

In what book does Marty make friends with Antoinette, even though they live on opposite sides of a fence?

In what book does a grandmother put a cooked onion plaster on Marty's mother's chest to help her recover from the Spanish flu?

In what book does Marty discover that Yuzy Kim, the Chinese washerman, is really a hatchet man for the tongs?

In what book do Marty's friends think she's awful because she walked through the town with an Indian girl?

In what book does a girl punch Freddy in the face when he plays post office at a birthday party?

Touch the Moon
Bauer, Marion Dane

In what book does Jennifer expect a real horse for her birthday, but gets riding lessons instead?

In what book does a tiny China horse come to life as a rather rude and self-centered stallion?

In what book does the horse remember his name is Moonseeker?

In what book is a girl invisible when riding her magic stallion?

In what book does Jennifer talk a horse out of a cave by pretending her flashlight is the moon?

Treasure Island
Stevenson, Robert Louis

In what book do Jim Hawkins, Dr. Livesy, and Squire Trelawney go hunting for treasure?

In which book does Jim Hawkins look forward to leaving the Admiral Benbow Inn and becoming a cabin boy?

In what book does the ship's cook turn out to be a pirate and a mutineer?

In what book does a boy overhear a plot about killing the squire, the doctor, and the captain?

In what book does John Silver knock out an honest sailor with his crutch and then stabs him to death?

Trouble with Tuck, The
Taylor, Theodore

In what book does a girl named Helen fall in love with a squirming, fat, yellow ball of fur given to her by her father?

In what book does a beautiful golden Labrador save a girl's life twice?

In what book does Helen's beautiful dog suddenly begin to go blind?

In what book does a girl become determined to find a solution to her dog's sudden blindness without breaking his spirit of independence?

In what book does Helen devote herself to not allowing her dog's blindness to end his life?

True Confessions of Charlotte Doyle, The
Avi

In what book does a young lady learn to climb the rigging, throw a knife, swab the deck, and scrape a hull?

In what book is the knife that a girl has been given used in a murder?

In what book does Zachariah tell a girl that they have two things in common? She's the only girl and he's the only black; he's the oldest and she's the youngest.

In what book does a girl discover that her loyalty should not be given to the captain, but rather to his crew?

In what book does the entire crew of a sailing ship sign on in order to get revenge?

Trumpet of the Swan, The
White, E. B.

In what book does Sam Beaver listen to the cygnets and realize that one is unable to speak?

In what book does Louis decide to find Sam so he can go to school with him?

In what book does a swan rescue a camper named Applegate?

In what book does a bird get a job as a bugler?

In which book does a bird earn over $4,000 to use to pay his debts?

Tuck Everlasting
Babbitt, Natalie

In what book does Winnie have to make a decision about whether or not to drink some water?

In what book is there a family that has lived forever?

In what book does Winnie help with a jail break to rescue her friend Mae?

In what book does a family move from place to place so that no one will notice that they never age?

In what book does Winnie pour magic water over her toad?

Twenty-One Balloons, The
Dubois, William

In what book does a professor find that his garbage works well as ballast for his balloon?

In which book does the professor's balloon contain chairs and tables made of balsa wood, paperback books printed in tiny type, a shark-fishing rod, and a mattress filled with gas?

In which book does a retired teacher, Professor Sherman, float into the greatest volcanic explosion in the world?

In what book does a professor land on the island of Krakatoa?

In what book does Mr. F. show a professor a diamond cave?

Up a Road Slowly
Hunt, Irene

In what book do the girls make Aggie be queen, so they won't have to sit with her at lunch?

In which book is Julie unhappy when she's sent to live with her Aunt Cordelia after her mother dies?

In what book does Aunt Cordelia give up teaching when the country school is closed?

In what book does a girl choose to live with her aunt even though it means she has little social life?

In what book does Julie discover that handsome Brett is only dating her so that she'll do his schoolwork for him?

Voyages of Dr. Doolittle, The
Lofting, Hugh

In what book do black parrots help three men in their fight against the Bagjagderags?

In what book does a fidgit tell the story of his thirteen months in an aquarium?

In what book was Tommy Stubbins delighted to be hired for two years as a doctor's assistant?

What book begins in the town of Puddleby-on-Marsh?

In what book is there a man who has written down the history of the monkeys?

Wait Till Helen Comes
Hahn, Mary Downing

In what book are Molly and Heather trapped in the cellar of a haunted house?

In what book do Molly and Michael investigate the legend of the haunted Harper house?

In what book does Molly's stepsister Heather become involved with a ghost child?

In what book is there a graveyard with a mysterious overgrown tombstone that bears the initials of a little girl?

In what book is Heather afraid that her father won't love her if he learns her secret about a long-ago fire?

Walking Stones, The
Hunter, Mollie

In what book does an old man use his gift of the Second Sight to prevent a hydroelectric dam from flooding the glen?

In what book does the Bodach foresee three men coming to the glen bringing a forest on the back of one, lightning in the hand of another, and death in the hand of the third?

In what book does the prehistoric circle of stones turn into a long line of white shapes who walk to a river?

What book tells of the clash between the electric power needs of modern humans and the ancient powers that reside in the Scottish hills?

In what book is there an old man with three important possessions: an old book of secret writings, a rope of cow hair, and a tall staff of bog oak?

War with Grandpa, The
Smith, Robert Kimmell

In what book did his grandfather hide Peter's monopoly pieces?

In which book does Peter want to keep his own room and not have a relative move in?

In which book does "the secret warrior" steal some slippers?

In which book do two people who love each other declare war just the same?

In what book does his grandfather hide Peter's toothbrush? He leaves a note telling Peter to use his finger.

Waterless Mountain
Armer, Laura

In what book does Younger Brother travel to the west to seek the Turquoise Woman?

In what book does a young Navaho learn to be a medicine man?

In what book does Pack Rat show Younger Brother a secret cave?

In what book does the word "jedi-be-toh" mean gasoline? Its literal translation means "automobile—its water."

In what book is a little boy taught by a Pack Rat?

Watership Down
Adams, Richard

In what book do some rabbits take care of a wounded gull named Kehaar?

In what book do the main characters speak the Lapine language? The author occasionally uses some of the words in the book.

In what book is there a final battle between General Woundwort and Bigwig?

In what book are some of the characters named Hazel, Fiver, Bigwig and Blackberry?

In what book do some rabbits search for a new warren?

Weasel
DeFelice, Cynthia

In what book does Nathan brood all winter about why he didn't kill his captor?

In what book is a stone wall used for messages and gifts such as medicine, moccasins, and seed corn?

Which book tells about the different paths taken by two Indian fighters? One adopts the ways of the Indian, while the other takes up killing the settlers and their animals.

In what book do two children follow a strange silent man who has their mother's gold locket?

In what book does Ezra save a man from losing his leg after he's been caught in an animal trap?

Westing Game, The
Raskin, Ellen

In which book does Turtle solve a mystery, but keeps the solution to herself?

In which book are sixteen heirs to a millionaire's fortune given some strange sets of clues?

In which book are six families mysteriously invited to buy six luxury apartments?

In which book are parts of a patriotic song used as clues to a mystery?

In which book does a millionaire pretend to be one of his heirs?

What Happened in Hamelin
Skurzynski, Gloria

In what book is a boy nicknamed Geist—meaning ghost—because he's usually covered with white flour?

In what book does Geist get together with a stranger named Gast?

In what book do rats in town carry the plague?

In what book does the stranger want Geist to mix rye-infected ergot in the sweetmeat buns he is baking?

In what book are children taken from a medieval town to be sold to a nobleman who lives far away?

Wheel on the School, The
DeJong, Meindert

In what book did Grandmother Sibble tell Lina of a long-ago time when their town had trees and storks?

In what book did the school have only five boys and one girl?

In what book did a group of children involve all the villagers in bringing the storks back to Shora?

In what book did Lina find an old wheel in an impossible place—under an old boat sunk in the sand?

In what book did slow, fat Eelka prove to be strong enough to rescue the biggest boy in the school?

When Hitler Stole Pink Rabbit
Kerr, Judith

In what book is a girl allowed to take only one toy animal with her on a trip?

In what book does Anna wonder if her Jewish family will ever be at home anywhere?

What book is about a little girl from Berlin, Germany? She travels to Switzerland, France, and England to escape the Nazis.

In what book were two children forbidden to play with Anna because she is Jewish?

In what book does a porter take a Jewish family to the wrong train in order to collect a bounty of a thousand marks?

Where the Red Fern Grows
Rawls, Wilson

In what book does Billy train his dogs to win a coon hunt contest?

In what book did Little Ann and Old Dan win a championship coon hunt?

What book is about a boy who receives a gold cup for winning a coon hunting contest with his two redbone hounds?

In what book are two hounds killed by a mountain lion?

In what book does a boy earn money to buy two hound dogs?

Whipping Boy, The
Fleischman, Sid

In which book is it forbidden for anyone to spank, thrash, or whack the prince?

In which book do two boys run away and end up being kidnapped by two outlaws?

In which book are two boys rescued from a thrashing by some outlaws when a girl sics her bear on them?

In which book do two boys make friends with a girl named Betsy and her dancing bear, Petunia?

In which book do Cutwater and Hold-Your-Nose-Billy kidnap two boys and hope to get a royal ransom?

White Seal, The
Kipling, Rudyard

In which book does a sea mammal try to find a safe place in the sea where men never come?

In which book does an animal find a safe island where the babies could be raised?

Which book is about an animal named Kotick?

In what book does Kotick watch his friends being killed for their skins?

In what book does Kotick have to fight the others in order to lead them to a safe place?

White Stag, The
Seredy, Kate

In what book does a vision of eagles and white herons cause a small boy to become blind?

In what book does a magic stag show the Huns the great land which is to become their home?

What book tells the legend of Attila the Conqueror, the Red Eagle?

In what book does the leader, the Red Eagle, find the legendary sword of Hador buried in the soil of the promised land?

In what book does a legendary male deer lead a tribe safely through the snow into a sheltered green valley?

Wind in the Willows, The
Grahame, Kenneth

In which book does Toad dress up as a washerwoman so he can escape from jail?

In what book are a mole and a toad among the major characters?

In what book do the field mice sing carols at Mole's End?

In what book does a mole get spring fever and stop his spring cleaning?

In which book does a mole learn to row a boat?

Winnie the Pooh
Milne, A. A.

In what book do a boy and a bear ride down a flooded river in an open upside-down umbrella?

In which book does a character live under the name of Sanders?

In what book does a toy bear hunt for honey in a bee tree?

In what book is there a very unhappy donkey named "Eeyore"?

In what book does a bear save himself from a flood by riding in an empty jug?

Winter Room, The
Paulsen, Gary

In which book does an old uncle tell tales of the old country and the new, until one of his nephews says he's a liar?

Which book tells of the joys and the hard times of living on a Minnesota farm?

In which book do the boys watch old Uncle David pick up an ax in each hand, raise both high over his head, and then swing them into the two ends of a log so that the wood splits clean and the axes meet in the middle?

In which book did Wayne try to jump from the barn onto the back of a draft horse just as his hero did in one of the Zane Grey books he was reading?

In which book does Crazy Alen play jokes on the foreman and keep on not only after he's fired, but even after he's dead?

Witch of Blackbird Pond, The
Speare, Elizabeth

What book tells about Quaker Hannah, Kit Tyler, Little Prudence, and Nathaniel Eaton?

In what book is it considered to be sinful to have a jack-o'-lantern?

In what book is the plague blamed on an old woman who lives by herself?

In what book is Kit thought to be a witch because she learned to swim when she lived in the Barbados?

In what book is Kit accused of witchcraft when she teaches a child to read the Bible?

Wright Brothers: How They Invented the Airplane, The
Freedman, Russell

In what book is an aircraft ground crew made up of men trained for water life saving?

In what book do two inventors own a printing press, a bicycle shop, and a dark room for photographic prints?

In what book do two men get a list from the weather bureau of the windiest places in the country?

What biography is illustrated by its subjects—men who lived at the beginning of the 1900s?

In what book does a mechanically minded mother make a sled for her sons?

Wrinkle in Time, A
L'Engle, Madeline

In what book does a disembodied, oversized brain give commands from a strange domed building?

In what book do Meg and Charles Wallace meet Mrs. Who, Mrs. Which, and Mrs. Whatsit?

In what book is the children's father captured by an evil brain?

In what book does Meg's love for her little brother, Charles Wallace, defeat the power of IT?

What is a tesseract? The definition is the name of this book.

Wrong Way Ragsdale
Hammer, Charles

In what book does a boy steal a vintage airplane because he wants to keep a rich man from taking it away from his father?

In what book do a boy and his sister spend several nights alone in the Ozark wilderness after crash-landing an airplane?

In what book do a boy and his sister survive several days in the wilderness by eating crawdads, perch, cattail roots and candy bars?

In what book does a little girl have an allergic reaction to eating the shellfish her brother caught while they were stranded?

In what book do a boy and girl discover some ancient Indian caves their father used to camp in when he was a boy?

Year of the Black Pony
Morey, Walt

In what book does a woman call her husband Mr. Shaw, instead of his first name of Frank?

In what book does the mother suggest a pebble in a horse's ear will keep it too busy to fight its rider?

In what book does a boy almost die getting a teddy bear for his sick sister?

What book is about Chris and Lucifer, the 4th of July bucking horse that "couldn't be broke"?

In what book does a woman insist that the man who caused her husband's death will have to marry her, since she can't support her family by herself?

Young Mac of Fort Vancouver
Carr, Mary Jane

In what book is a boy kidnapped by an Indian Medicine Man because Three Gulls is jealous of his spirit?

What book is about a boy who is half-Scotch, and half-Indian, who is sent out to a Hudson's Bay Post to stay with Dr. John McLoughlin?

In what book is young Donald given the Northman's feather of courage by the Voyagers of the York Factory Express?

In what book does Donald rescue a white child, Mia, from the Indians?

In what book does the schoolmaster make the boy with the worst marks of the week in school wear a rusty gunlock around his neck?

Appendices

Author List

Author	Title
Adams, Richard	Watership Down
Adler, Susan	Meet Samantha
Alcott, Louisa May	Little Men
Alcott, Louisa May	Little Women
Alexander, Lloyd	Book of Three, The
Alexander, Lloyd	High King, The
Anderson, C. W.	Blind Connemara, The
Anderson, Margaret	Searching for Shona
Armer, Laura	Waterless Mountain
Armstrong, William	Sounder
Atwater, Richard	Mr. Popper's Penguins
Avi	True Confessions of Charlotte Doyle, The
Babbitt, Natalie	Tuck Everlasting
Bailey, Carolyn	Miss Hickory
Ball, Zachary	Bristle Face
Banks, Lynn Reid	Indian in the Cupboard, The

Author	Title
Barrie, J. M.	Peter Pan
Bauer, Marion Dane	On My Honor
Bauer, Marion Dane	Touch the Moon
Beatty, Patricia	Lacy Makes a Match
Binns, Archie	Sea Pup
Blos, Joan	Gathering of Days, A
Blume, Judy	Just As Long As We're Together
Blume, Judy	Superfudge
Blume, Judy	Tales of a Fourth Grade Nothing
Bond, Michael	Bear Called Paddington, A
Bond, Michael	Tales of Olga Da Polga, The
Bonham, Frank	Rascals from Haskells Gym, The
Brink, Carol R.	Caddie Woodlawn
Bulla, Clyde	Shoeshine Girl
Burch, Robert	Ida Early Comes over the Mountain
Burnett, Frances H.	Secret Garden, The
Burnford, Sheila	Incredible Journey, The
Butterworth, Oliver	Enormous Egg, The
Byars, Betsy	Blossoms and the Green Phantom, The
Byars, Betsy	Computer Nut, The
Byars, Betsy	Cybil War, The
Byars, Betsy	Not Just Anybody Family, The
Byars, Betsy	Pinballs, The
Byars, Betsy	Summer of the Swans
Calhoun, Mary	Katie John
Callen, Larry	Pinch
Carr, Mary Jane	Young Mac of Fort Vancouver
Carroll, Lewis	Alice's Adventures in Wonderland
Caudill, Rebecca	Did You Carry the Flag Today, Charlie?
Clark, Ann Nolan	Secret of the Andes
Cleary, Beverly	Dear Mr. Henshaw
Cleary, Beverly	Henry Huggins
Cleary, Beverly	Mouse and the Motorcycle, The

Author	Title
Cleary, Beverly	Ramona and Her Father
Cleary, Beverly	Ramona Forever
Cleary, Beverly	Ramona Quimby, Age 8
Coatsworth, Elizabeth	Cat Who Went to Heaven, The
Cohen, Barbara	Molly's Pilgrim
Collodi, Carlo	Adventures of Pinocchio, The
Cone, Molly	Amazing Memory of Harvey Bean, The
Conford, Ellen	Luck of Pokey Bloom, The
Conrad, Pam	My Daniel
Cooper, Susan	Grey King, The
Cooper, Susan	Over Sea, under Stone
Corbett, Scott	Limerick Trick, The
Corbin, William	Golden Mare, The
Corbin, William	Smoke
Coville, Bruce	Jeremy Thatcher, Dragon Hatcher
Crayder, Dorothy	Ishkabibble
Dahl, Roald	Charlie and the Chocolate Factory
Dahl, Roald	Danny the Champion of the World
Dahl, Roald	James and the Giant Peach
Danziger, Paula	Cat Ate My Gymsuit, The
Daugherty, James	Daniel Boone
De Angeli, Marguerite	Door in the Wall
De Clements, Barthe	Sixth Grade Can Really Kill You
De Roo, Anne	Scrub Fire
DeFelice, Cynthia	Weasel
DeJong, Meindert	Wheel on the School, The
Dubois, William	Twenty-One Balloons, The
Eager, Edward	Half Magic
Edmonds, Walter	Matchlock Gun, The
Enright, Elizabeth	Thimble Summer
Estes, Eleanor	Ginger Pye
Farley, Walter	Black Stallion, The
Fitzgerald, John D.	Great Brain, The

Author	Title
Fitzhugh, Louise	Harriet the Spy
Fleischman, Paul	Joyful Noise: Poems for Two Voices
Fleischman, Sid	Whipping Boy, The
Fleming, Ian	Chitty Chitty Bang Bang
Forbes, Esther	Johnny Tremain
Fox, Paula	Slave Dancer, The
Frazier, Neta	Stout-Hearted Seven, The
Freedman, Russell	Lincoln: A Photobiography
Freedman, Russell	Wright Brothers: How They Invented the Airplane, The
Gardiner, John	Stone Fox
Garst, Shannon	Cowboy Boots
George, Jean	Julie of the Wolves
George, Jean	My Side of the Mountain
Gilson, Jamie	Hello, My Name Is Scrambled Eggs
Gilson, Jamie	Thirteen Ways to Sink a Sub
Gipson, Fred	Old Yeller
Gordon, Shirley	Boy Who Wanted a Family, The
Graeber, Charlotte Towner	Grey Cloud
Grahame, Kenneth	Reluctant Dragon, The
Grahame, Kenneth	Wind in the Willows, The
Gray, Elizabeth	Adam of the Road
Greene, Bette	Philip Hall Likes Me I Reckon, Maybe
Greenwald, Sheila	Give Us a Great Big Smile Rosy Cole
Greenwald, Sheila	Mariah Delaney Lending Library Disaster, The
Gregory, Kristiana	Legend of Jimmy Spoon, The
Haas, Dorothy	Secret Life of Dilly McBean, The
Hahn, Mary Downing	Wait Till Helen Comes
Hamilton, Virginia	M. C. Higgins the Great
Hammer, Charles	Wrong Way Ragsdale
Hautzig, Esther	Endless Steppe, The
Haywood, Carolyn	"B" Is for Betsy
Haywood, Carolyn	"C" Is for Cupcake

Author	Title
Hendry, Frances	Quest for a Maid
Henry, Marguerite	King of the Wind
Henry, Marguerite	Misty of Chincoteague
Hicks, Clifford	Alvin's Secret Code
Hicks, Clifford	Peter Potts
Holling, Holling C.	Paddle-to-the-Sea
Howard, Ellen	Edith Herself
Howe, Deborah	Bunnicula
Hunt, Irene	Across Five Aprils
Hunt, Irene	Up a Road Slowly
Hunter, Mollie	Walking Stones, The
Hurmence, Belinda	Girl Called Boy, A
Hurwitz, Johanna	Russell Sprouts
Hyde, Dayton	Island of the Loons, The
Jacques, Brian	Redwall
James, Will	Smoky the Cow Horse
Joyce, Susan	Peel the Extraordinary Elephant
Jukes, Mavis	Like Jake and Me
Juster, Norton	Phantom Tollbooth, The
Kastner, Erick	Little Man, The
Keith, Harold	Rifles for Watie
Kerr, Judith	When Hitler Stole Pink Rabbit
Key, Alexander	Escape to Witch Mountain
King-Smith, Dick	Babe; The Gallant Pig
Kipling, Rudyard	Rikki Tikki Tavi
Kipling, Rudyard	White Seal, The
Kjelgaard, Jim	Big Red
Kjelgaard, Jim	Haunt Fox
Knight, Eric	Lassie Come Home
Konigsburg, E. L.	From the Mixed Up Files of Mrs. Basil E. Frankweiler
Konigsburg, E. L.	Journey to an 800 Number
Krumgold, Joseph	. . . And Now, Miguel

Author	Title
L'Engle, Madeline	Wrinkle in Time, A
Lampman, Evelyn Sibley	Three Knocks on the Wall
Langton, Jane	Fledgling, The
Lawson, Robert	Rabbit Hill
Lenski, Lois	Strawberry Girl
Lester, Julius	Tales of Uncle Remus, The
LeVoy, Myron	Magic Hat of Mortimer Wintergreen, The
Lewis, C. S.	Lion, the Witch and the Wardrobe, The
Lindgren, Astrid	Pippi Longstocking
Lindquist, Jennie	Golden Name Day, The
Lisle, Janet Taylor	Afternoon of the Elves
Lofting, Hugh	Story of Dr. Doolittle, The
Lofting, Hugh	Voyages of Dr. Doolittle, The
London, Jack	Call of the Wild, The
Lord, Bette	In the Year of the Boar and Jackie Robinson
Lowry, Lois	Number the Stars
Lowry, Lois	Switcharound
MacDonald, Betty	Hello, Mrs. Piggle Wiggle
MacDonald, Betty	Mrs. Piggle Wiggle
MacGregor, Ellen	Miss Pickerell Goes to Mars
MacKellar, William	Smallest Monster in the World, The
MacLachlan, Patricia	Sarah Plain and Tall
Martin, Ann	Ten Kids, No Pets
McCaffrey, Anne	Dragonsong
McCloskey, Robert	Homer Price
McCormick, Dell	Paul Bunyan Swings His Axe
McKinley, Robin	Hero and the Crown, The
McKissick, Patricia	Dark-Thirty: Tales of the Supernatural, The
McSwigan, Marie	Snow Treasure
Meigs, Cornelia	Invincible Louisa
Merrill, Jean	Pushcart War, The
Meyers, Franklyn	Me and Caleb
Milne, A. A.	Winnie the Pooh

Author	Title
Moeri, Louise	Save Queen of Sheba
Monjo, F. N.	Letters to Horseface
Montgomery, L. M.	Anne of Green Gables
Morey, Walt	Angry Waters
Morey, Walt	Gentle Ben
Morey, Walt	Gloomy Gus
Morey, Walt	Year of the Black Pony
Morrow, Honore	On to Oregon
Mowat, Farley	Owls in the Family
Naylor, Phyllis	Shiloh
Neville, Emily	It's Like This, Cat
North, Sterling	Rascal
Norton, Mary	Borrowers, The
Nostlinger, Christine	Konrad
O'Brien, Robert	Mrs. Frisby and the Rats of NIMH
O'Dell, Scott	Island of the Blue Dolphins
Park, Barbara	Kid in the Red Jacket, The
Paterson, Katherine	Bridge to Terabithia
Paulsen, Gary	Hatchet
Paulsen, Gary	Winter Room, The
Peck Robert	Soup and Me
Pyle, Howard	Story of King Arthur and His Knights, The
Raskin, Ellen	Westing Game, The
Rawls, Wilson	Summer of the Monkeys
Rawls, Wilson	Where the Red Fern Grows
Roberts, Willo Davis	Megan's Island
Robertson, Keith	Henry Reed, Inc.
Rockwell, Thomas	How to Eat Fried Worms
Rodgers, Mary	Freaky Friday
Rylant, Cynthia	Blue-Eyed Daisy, A
Rylant, Cynthia	Missing May
Sachar, Louis	There's a Boy in the Girl's Bathroom
Sachs, Marilyn	Bear's House, The

Author	Title
Sachs, Marilyn	Secret Friend, A
Saint-Exupery, Antoine De	Little Prince, The
Salten, Felix	Bambi
Selden, George	Cricket in Times Square, The
Seredy, Kate	White Stag, The
Sewell, Anna	Black Beauty
Sharmat, Marjorie	Getting Something on Maggie Marmelstein
Skurzynski, Gloria	What Happened in Hamelin
Smith, Dodie	101 Dalmations
Smith, Robert Kimmell	War with Grandpa, The
Snyder, Zilpha Keatley	And Condors Danced
Sorensen, Virginia	Miracles on Maple Hill
Speare, Elizabeth	Bronze Bow, The
Speare, Elizabeth	Sign of the Beaver, The
Speare, Elizabeth	Witch of Blackbird Pond, The
Sperry, Armstrong	Call It Courage
Spinelli, Jerry	Maniac Magee
Spyri, Johanna	Heidi
Stanley, Jerry	Children of the Dust Bowl
Steele, William O.	Lone Hunt, The
Steig, William	Abel's Island
Stevenson, Robert Louis	Treasure Island
Stolz, Mary	Explorer of Barkham Street, The
Taylor, Mildred	Roll of Thunder, Hear My Cry
Taylor, Sydney	All of a Kind Family
Taylor, Theodore	Trouble with Tuck, The
Tolkien, J. R.	Hobbit, The
Travers, P. L.	Mary Poppins
Tregaskis, Richard	John F. Kennedy and P.T. 109
Twain, Mark	Adventures of Tom Sawyer, The
Uchida, Yoshito	Journey to Topaz
Van Leeuwen, Jean	Benjy, the Football Hero
Van Leeuwen, Jean	Great Rescue Operation, The
Voigt, Cynthia	Building Blocks

Author	Title
Voigt, Cynthia	Dicey's Song
Voigt, Cynthia	Homecoming
Wallace, Bill	Danger in Quicksand Swamp
Wallace, Bill	Beauty
White, E. B.	Charlotte's Web
White, E. B.	Stuart Little
White, E. B.	Trumpet of the Swan, The
Wilder, Laura Ingalls	By the Shores of Silver Lake
Wilder, Laura Ingalls	Little House in the Big Woods
Williams, Jay	Danny Dunn and the Homework Machine
Winthrop, Elizabeth	Castle in the Attic, The
Wrede, Patricia	Dealing with Dragons
Wright, Betty Ren	Dollhouse Murders, The
Wyss, J. R.	Swiss Family Robinson, The
Yates, Elizabeth	Amos Fortune, Free Man
Yolen, Jane	Boy Who Spoke Chimp, The

Easier Books
INTEREST AND/OR READING LEVEL
ALSO USEFUL FOR GRADE 3

Title	Author
101 Dalmations	Smith, Dodie
All of a Kind Family	Taylor, Sydney
Alvin's Secret Code	Hicks, Clifford
Amazing Memory of Harvey Bean, The	Cone, Molly
"B" Is for Betsy	Haywood, Carolyn
Babe; The Gallant Pig	King-Smith, Dick
Bear Called Paddington, A	Bond, Michael
Blind Connemara, The	Anderson, C. W.
Boy Who Spoke Chimp, The	Yolen, Jane
Boy Who Wanted a Family, The	Gordon, Shirley
Bristle Face	Ball, Zachary

Title	Author
"C" Is for Cupcake	Haywood, Carolyn
Call It Courage	Sperry, Armstrong
Computer Nut, The	Byars, Betsy
Cricket in Times Square, The	Selden, George
Danny Dunn and the Homework Machine	Williams, Jay
Dear Mr. Henshaw	Cleary, Beverly
Did You Carry the Flag Today, Charlie?	Caudill, Rebecca
Give Us a Great Big Smile Rosy Cole	Greenwald, Sheila
Golden Mare, The	Corbin, William
Golden Name Day, The	Lindquist, Jennie
Great Rescue Operation, The	Van Leeuwen, Jean
Hello, Mrs. Piggle Wiggle	MacDonald, Betty
Homer Price	McCloskey, Robert
How to Eat Fried Worms	Rockwell, Thomas
Ida Early Comes over the Mountain	Burch, Robert
Ishkabibble	Crayder, Dorothy
Katie John	Calhoun, Mary
Kid in the Red Jacket, The	Park, Barbara
Lion, the Witch and the Wardrobe, The	Lewis, C. S.
Mariah Delaney Lending Library Disaster, The	Greenwald, Sheila
Meet Samantha	Adler, Susan
Miss Pickerell Goes to Mars	MacGregor, Ellen
Molly's Pilgrim	Cohen, Barbara
Paul Bunyan Swings His Axe	McCormick, Dell
Peel the Extraordinary Elephant	Joyce, Susan
Peter Potts	Hicks, Clifford
Pippi Longstocking	Lindgren, Astrid
Ramona and Her Father	Cleary, Beverly
Ramona Forever	Cleary, Beverly
Rikki Tikki Tavi	Kipling, Rudyard
Russell Sprouts	Hurwitz, Johanna
Secret Friend, A	Sachs, Marilyn
Shoeshine Girl	Bulla, Clyde

Title	Author
Strawberry Girl	Lenski, Lois
Superfudge	Blume, Judy
Tales of a Fourth Grade Nothing	Blume, Judy
Ten Kids, No Pets	Martin, Ann
Touch the Moon	Bauer, Marion Dane
White Seal, The	Kipling, Rudyard
Winnie the Pooh	Milne, A. A.

More Advanced Books
ALSO USEFUL FOR MIDDLE AND
JUNIOR HIGH SCHOOLS

Title	Author
Across Five Aprils	Hunt, Irene
Amos Fortune, Free Man	Yates, Elizabeth
. . . And Now, Miguel	Krumgold, Joseph
Angry Waters	Morey, Walt
Bambi	Salten, Felix
Bear's House, The	Sachs, Marilyn
Big Red	Kjelgaard, Jim
Blue-Eyed Daisy, A	Rylant, Cynthia
Book of Three, The	Alexander, Lloyd
Building Blocks	Voigt, Cynthia
Cat Ate My Gymsuit, The	Danziger, Paula
Children of the Dust Bowl	Stanley, Jerry
Cybil War, The	Byars, Betsy
Daniel Boone	Daugherty, James
Danny the Champion of the World	Dahl, Roald
Dicey's Song	Voigt, Cynthia
Dollhouse Murders, The	Wright, Betty Ren
Door in the Wall	De Angeli, Marguerite
Dragonsong	McCaffrey, Anne

Title	Author
Edith Herself	Howard, Ellen
Endless Steppe, The	Hautzig, Esther
Escape to Witch Mountain	Key, Alexander
Explorer of Barkham Street, The	Stolz, Mary
Gathering of Days, A	Blos, Joan
Grey King, The	Cooper, Susan
Harriet the Spy	Fitzhugh, Louise
Hatchet	Paulsen, Gary
Hero and the Crown, The	McKinley, Robin
Hobbit, The	Tolkien, J. R.
Homecoming	Voigt, Cynthia
In the Year of the Boar and Jackie Robinson	Lord, Bette
Incredible Journey, The	Burnford, Sheila
Island of the Loons, The	Hyde, Dayton
It's Like This, Cat	Neville, Emily
John F. Kennedy and P.T. 109	Tregaskis, Richard
Johnny Tremain	Forbes, Esther
Journey to an 800 Number	Konigsburg, E. L.
Just as Long as We're Together	Blume, Judy
Lincoln: A Photobiography	Freedman, Russell
Little Women	Alcott, Louisa May
M. C. Higgins the Great	Hamilton, Virginia
Miracles on Maple Hill	Sorensen, Virginia
Missing May	Rylant, Cynthia
My Daniel	Conrad, Pam
Number the Stars	Lowry, Lois
Over Sea, under Stone	Cooper, Susan
Pinballs, The	Byars, Betsy
Quest for a Maid	Hendry, Frances
Rascal	North, Sterling
Rascals from Haskells Gym, The	Bonham, Frank
Roll of Thunder, Hear My Cry	Taylor, Mildred
Searching for Shona	Anderson, Margaret

Title	Author
Sixth Grade Can Really Kill You	De Clements, Barthe
Slave Dancer, The	Fox, Paula
Smoke	Corbin, William
Switcharound	Lowry, Lois
Three Knocks on the Wall	Lampman, Evelyn Sibley
Up a Road Slowly	Hunt, Irene
Wait Till Helen Comes	Hahn, Mary Downing
Watership Down	Adams, Richard
Westing Game, The	Raskin, Ellen
What Happened in Hamelin	Skurzynski, Gloria
Wheel on the School, The	DeJong, Meindert
Whipping Boy, The	Fleischman, Sid
Winter Room, The	Paulson, Gary

Animals

Title	Author
101 Dalmations	Smith, Dodie
Abel's Island	Steig, William
Babe; The Gallant Pig	King-Smith, Dick
Bambi	Salten, Felix
Bear Called Paddington, A	Bond, Michael
Beauty	Wallace, Bill
Big Red	Kjelgaard, Jim
Black Beauty	Sewell, Anna
Black Stallion, The	Farley, Walter
Blind Connemara, The	Anderson, C. W.
Bristle Face	Ball, Zachary
Bunnicula	Howe, Deborah
"C" Is for Cupcake	Haywood, Carolyn
Call of the Wild, The	London, Jack

Title	Author
Cat Who Went to Heaven, The	Coatsworth, Elizabeth
Charlotte's Web	White, E. B.
Cricket in Times Square, The	Selden, George
Enormous Egg, The	Butterworth, Oliver
Fledgling, The	Langton, Jane
Gentle Ben	Morey, Walt
Ginger Pye	Estes, Eleanor
Gloomy Gus	Morey, Walt
Golden Mare, The	Corbin, William
Great Rescue Operation, The	Van Leeuwen, Jean
Grey Cloud	Graeber, Charlotte Towner
Haunt Fox	Kjelgaard, Jim
Incredible Journey, The	Burnford, Sheila
It's Like This, Cat	Neville, Emily
Julie of the Wolves	George, Jean
King of the Wind	Henry, Marguerite
Lassie Come Home	Knight, Eric
Misty of Chincoteague	Henry, Marguerite
Mouse and the Motorcycle, The	Cleary, Beverly
Mr. Popper's Penguins	Atwater, Richard
Mrs. Frisby and the Rats of NIMH	O'Brien, Robert
Owls in the Family	Mowat, Farley
Peel the Extraordinary Elephant	Joyce, Susan
Pinch	Callen, Larry
Rabbit Hill	Lawson, Robert
Rascal	North, Sterling
Redwall	Jacques, Brian
Rikki Tikki Tavi	Kipling, Rudyard
Sea Pup	Binns, Archie
Shiloh	Naylor, Phyllis
Smoke	Corbin, William
Smoky the Cow Horse	James, Will
Sounder	Armstrong, William

Title	Author
Story of Dr. Doolittle, The	Lofting, Hugh
Stuart Little	White, E. B.
Tales of Olga Da Polga, The	Bond, Michael
Tales of Uncle Remus, The	Lester, Julius
Touch the Moon	Bauer, Marion Dane
Trouble with Tuck, The	Taylor, Theodore
Trumpet of the Swan, The	White, E. B.
War with Grandpa, The	Smith, Robert Kimmell
Watership Down	Adams, Richard
Where the Red Fern Grows	Rawls, Wilson
White Seal, The	Kipling, Rudyard
Wind in the Willows, The	Grahame, Kenneth
Year of the Black Pony	Morey, Walt

Historical Settings

Title	Author
Across Five Aprils	Hunt, Irene
Adam of the Road	Gray, Elizabeth
Adventures of Tom Sawyer, The	Twain, Mark
All of a Kind Family	Taylor, Sydney
Amos Fortune, Free Man	Yates, Elizabeth
And Condors Danced	Snyder, Zilpha Keatley
Bronze Bow, The	Speare, Elizabeth
By the Shores of Silver Lake	Wilder, Laura Ingalls
Caddie Woodlawn	Brink, Carol R.
Children of the Dust Bowl	Stanley, Jerry
Cowboy Boots	Garst, Shannon
Daniel Boone	Daugherty, James
Door in the Wall	De Angeli, Marguerite
Endless Steppe, The	Hautzig, Esther
Gathering of Days, A	Blos, Joan

Title	Author
Girl Called Boy, A	Hurmence, Belinda
Invincible Louisa	Meigs, Cornelia
Johnny Tremain	Forbes, Esther
Journey to Topaz	Uchida, Yoshito
Lacy Makes a Match	Beatty, Patricia
Legend of Jimmy Spoon, The	Gregory, Kristiana
Letters to Horseface	Monjo, F. N.
Lincoln: A Photobiography	Freedman, Russell
Little House in the Big Woods	Wilder, Laura Ingalls
Lone Hunt, The	Steele, William O.
Matchlock Gun, The	Edmonds, Walter
Meet Samantha	Adler, Susan
Molly's Pilgrim	Cohen, Barbara
Number the Stars	Lowry, Lois
On to Oregon	Morrow, Honore
Quest for a Maid	Hendry, Frances
Rifles for Watie	Keith, Harold
Roll of Thunder, Hear My Cry	Taylor, Mildred
Sarah Plain and Tall	MacLachlan, Patricia
Save Queen of Sheba	Moeri, Louise
Sign of the Beaver, The	Speare, Elizabeth
Slave Dancer, The	Fox, Paula
Snow Treasure	McSwigan, Marie
Sounder	Armstrong, William
Stout-Hearted Seven, The	Frazier, Neta
True Confessions of Charlotte Doyle, The	Avi
Weasel	DeFelice, Cynthia
What Happened in Hamelin	Skurzynski, Gloria
When Hitler Stole Pink Rabbit	Kerr, Judith
Witch of Blackbird Pond, The	Speare, Elizabeth
Wright Brothers: How They Invented the Airplane, The	Freedman, Russell
Young Mac of Fort Vancouver	Carr, Mary Jane

Classics: Old and New

Title	Author
Adventures of Pinocchio, The	Collodi, Carlo
Adventures of Tom Sawyer, The	Twain, Mark
Alice's Adventures in Wonderland	Carroll, Lewis
Anne of Green Gables	Montgomery, L. M.
Bambi	Salten, Felix
Black Beauty	Sewell, Anna
Black Stallion, The	Farley, Walter
Borrowers, The	Norton, Mary
Caddie Woodlawn	Brink, Carol R.
Call of the Wild, The	London, Jack
Charlotte's Web	White, E. B.
Half Magic	Eager, Edward
Heidi	Spyri, Johanna
Hobbit, The	Tolkien, J. R.
Island of the Blue Dolphins	O'Dell, Scott
James and the Giant Peach	Dahl, Roald
Lassie Come Home	Knight, Eric
Lion, the Witch and the Wardrobe, The	Lewis, C. S.
Little House in the Big Woods	Wilder, Laura Ingalls
Little Men	Alcott, Louisa May
Little Prince, The	Saint-Exupery, Antoine De
Little Women	Alcott, Louisa May
Mary Poppins	Travers, P. L.
Miss Hickory	Bailey, Carolyn
Misty of Chincoteague	Henry, Marguerite
Mrs. Frisby and the Rats of NIMH	O'Brien, Robert
Mrs. Piggle Wiggle	MacDonald, Betty
My Side of the Mountain	George, Jean
Old Yeller	Gipson, Fred
Paddle-to-the-Sea	Holling, Holling C.
Paul Bunyan Swings His Axe	McCormick, Dell

Title	Author
Peter Pan	Barrie, J. M.
Phantom Tollbooth, The	Juster, Norton
Pippi Longstocking	Lindgren, Astrid
Rabbit Hill	Lawson, Robert
Reluctant Dragon, The	Grahame, Kenneth
Secret Garden, The	Burnett, Frances H.
Secret of the Andes	Clark, Ann Nolan
Story of Dr. Doolittle, The	Lofting, Hugh
Story of King Arthur and His Knights, The	Pyle, Howard
Swiss Family Robinson, The	Wyss, J. R.
Tales of Uncle Remus, The	Lester, Julius
Treasure Island	Stevenson, Robert Louis
Trumpet of the Swan, The	White, E. B.
Tuck Everlasting	Babbitt, Natalie
Voyages of Dr. Doolittle, The	Lofting, Hugh
Where the Red Fern Grows	Rawls, Wilson
Wind in the Willows, The	Grahame, Kenneth
Winnie the Pooh	Milne, A. A.

Humor

Title	Author
All of a Kind Family	Taylor, Sydney
Amazing Memory of Harvey Bean, The	Cone, Molly
Babe; The Gallant Pig	King-Smith, Dick
Benjy, the Football Hero	Van Leeuwen, Jean
Blossoms and the Green Phantom, The	Byars, Betsy
Cybil War, The	Byars, Betsy
Danny Dunn and the Homework Machine	Williams, Jay
Danny the Champion of the World	Dahl, Roald
Did You Carry the Flag Today, Charlie?	Caudill, Rebecca

Title	Author
Enormous Egg, The	Butterworth, Oliver
Freaky Friday	Rodgers, Mary
Getting Something on Maggie Marmelstein	Sharmat, Marjorie
Give Us a Great Big Smile Rosy Cole	Greenwald, Sheila
Great Brain, The	Fitzgerald, John D.
Great Rescue Operation, The	Van Leeuwen, Jean
Harriet the Spy	Fitzhugh, Louise
Hello, Mrs. Piggle Wiggle	MacDonald, Betty
Hello, My Name Is Scrambled Eggs	Gilson, Jamie
Henry Huggins	Cleary, Beverly
Henry Reed, Inc.	Robertson, Keith
Homer Price	McCloskey, Robert
How to Eat Fried Worms	Rockwell, Thomas
Ida Early Comes over the Mountain	Burch, Robert
Ishkabibble	Crayder, Dorothy
Katie John	Calhoun, Mary
Lacy Makes a Match	Beatty, Patricia
Luck of Pokey Bloom, The	Conford, Ellen
Maniac Magee	Spinelli, Jerry
Mariah Delaney Lending Library Disaster, The	Greenwald, Sheila
Me and Caleb	Meyers, Franklyn
Mouse and the Motorcycle, The	Cleary, Beverly
Mr. Popper's Penguins	Atwater, Richard
Mrs. Piggle Wiggle	MacDonald, Betty
Not Just Anybody Family, The	Byars, Betsy
Owls in the Family	Mowat, Farley
Peter Potts	Hicks, Clifford
Philip Hall Likes Me I Reckon, Maybe	Greene, Bette
Pippi Longstocking	Lindgren, Astrid
Pushcart War, The	Merrill, Jean
Ramona and Her Father	Cleary, Beverly
Ramona Forever	Cleary, Beverly
Ramona Quimby, Age 8	Cleary, Beverly

Title	Author
Russell Sprouts	Hurwitz, Johanna
Soup and Me	Peck, Robert
Summer of the Monkeys	Rawls, Wilson
Superfudge	Blume, Judy
Switcharound	Lowry, Lois
Tales of a Fourth Grade Nothing	Blume, Judy
There's a Boy in the Girl's Bathroom	Sachar, Louis
Thirteen Ways to Sink a Sub	Gilson, Jamie
War with Grandpa, The	Smith, Robert Kimmell

Mystery and Adventure

Title	Author
101 Dalmations	Smith, Dodie
Abel's Island	Steig, William
Across Five Aprils	Hunt, Irene
Adam of the Road	Gray, Elizabeth
Alvin's Secret Code	Hicks, Clifford
Angry Waters	Morey, Walt
Boy Who Spoke Chimp, The	Yolen, Jane
Call It Courage	Sperry, Armstrong
Call of the Wild, The	London, Jack
Danger in Quicksand Swamp	Wallace, Bill
Dollhouse Murders, The	Wright, Betty Ren
From the Mixed Up Files of Mrs. Basil E. Frankweiler	Konigsburg, E. L.
Gentle Ben	Morey, Walt
Girl Called Boy, A	Hurmence, Belinda
Gloomy Gus	Morey, Walt
Hatchet	Paulsen, Gary
Haunt Fox	Kjelgaard, Jim
Island of the Loons, The	Hyde, Dayton

Title	Author
John F. Kennedy and P.T. 109	Tregaskis, Richard
Journey to an 800 Number	Konigsburg, E. L.
Julie of the Wolves	George, Jean
Legend of Jimmy Spoon, The	Gregory, Kristiana
Little Man, The	Kastner, Erick
Magic Hat of Mortimer Wintergreen, The	LeVoy, Myron
Me and Caleb	Meyers, Franklyn
Megan's Island	Roberts, Willo Davis
My Daniel	Conrad, Pam
My Side of the Mountain	George, Jean
Paddle-to-the-Sea	Holling, Holling C.
Scrub Fire	De Roo, Anne
Searching for Shona	Anderson, Margaret
Secret Life of Dilly McBean, The	Haas, Dorothy
Stone Fox	Gardiner, John
Summer of the Monkeys	Rawls, Wilson
Treasure Island	Stevenson, Robert Louis
Twenty-One Balloons, The	DuBois, William
Voyages of Dr. Doolittle, The	Lofting, Hugh
Weasel	DeFelice, Cynthia
Westing Game, The	Raskin, Ellen
Wheel on the School, The	DeJong, Meindert
Whipping Boy, The	Fleischman, Sid
Wrong Way Ragsdale	Hammer, Charles
Year of the Black Pony	Morey, Walt

Fantasy and Magic

Title	Author
Afternoon of the Elves	Lisle, Janet Taylor
Alice's Adventures in Wonderland	Carroll, Lewis
Book of Three, The	Alexander, Lloyd

Title	Author
Borrowers, The	Norton, Mary
Castle in the Attic, The	Winthrop, Elizabeth
Charlie and the Chocolate Factory	Dahl, Roald
Chitty Chitty Bang Bang	Fleming, Ian
Computer Nut, The	Byars, Betsy
Dark-Thirty: Tales of the Supernatural, The	McKissack, Patricia
Dealing with Dragons	Wrede, Patricia
Dragonsong	McCaffrey, Anne
Escape to Witch Mountain	Key, Alexander
Fledgling, The	Langton, Jane
Freaky Friday	Rodgers, Mary
Grey King, The	Cooper, Susan
Half Magic	Eager, Edward
Hero and the Crown, The	McKinley, Robin
High King, The	Alexander, Lloyd
Hobbit, The	Tolkien, J. R.
Indian in the Cupboard, The	Banks, Lynn Reid
James and the Giant Peach	Dahl, Roald
Jeremy Thatcher, Dragon Hatcher	Coville, Bruce
Konrad	Nostlinger, Christine
Limerick Trick, The	Corbett, Scott
Lion, the Witch and the Wardrobe, The	Lewis, C. S.
Little Man, The	Kastner, Erick
Little Prince, The	Saint-Exupery, Antoine De
Magic Hat of Mortimer Wintergreen, The	LeVoy, Myron
Mary Poppins	Travers, P. L.
Miss Pickerell Goes to Mars	MacGregor, Ellen
Over Sea, under Stone	Cooper, Susan
Peter Pan	Barrie, J. M.
Phantom Tollbooth, The	Juster, Norton
Redwall	Jacques, Brian
Secret Life of Dilly McBean, The	Haas, Dorothy
Smallest Monster in the World, The	MacKellar, William

Title	Author
Stuart Little	White, E. B.
Tuck Everlasting	Babbitt, Natalie
Walking Stones, The	Hunter, Mollie
White Stag, The	Seredy, Kate
Wrinkle in Time, A	L'Engle, Madeline

Newbery Award and Honor Books

Title	Author
Abel's Island	Steig, William
Across Five Aprils	Hunt, Irene
Adam of the Road	Gray, Elizabeth
Afternoon of the Elves	Lisle, Janet Taylor
Amos Fortune, Free Man	Yates, Elizabeth
. . . And Now, Miguel	Krumgold, Joseph
Bridge to Terabithia	Paterson, Katherine
Bronze Bow, The	Speare, Elizabeth
By the Shores of Silver Lake	Wilder, Laura Ingalls
Caddie Woodlawn	Brink, Carol R.
Call It Courage	Sperry, Armstrong
Cat Who Went to Heaven, The	Coatsworth, Elizabeth
Charlotte's Web	White, E. B.
Cricket in Times Square, The	Selden, George
Daniel Boone	Daugherty, James
Dark-Thirty: Tales of the Supernatural, The	McKissack, Patricia
Dear Mr. Henshaw	Cleary, Beverly
Dicey's Song	Voigt, Cynthia
Door in the Wall	De Angeli, Marguerite
Fledgling, The	Langton, Jane
From the Mixed Up Files of Mrs. Basil E. Frankweiler	Konigsburg, E. L.

Title	Author
Gathering of Days, A	Blos, Joan
Ginger Pye	Estes, Eleanor
Golden Name Day, The	Lindquist, Jennie
Grey King, The	Cooper, Susan
Hatchet	Paulsen, Gary
Hero and the Crown, The	McKinley, Robin
High King, The	Alexander, Lloyd
Invincible Louisa	Meigs, Cornelia
Island of the Blue Dolphins	O'Dell, Scott
It's Like This, Cat	Neville, Emily
Johnny Tremain	Forbes, Esther
Joyful Noise: Poems for Two Voices	Fleischman, Paul
Julie of the Wolves	George, Jean
King of the Wind	Henry, Marguerite
Lincoln: A Photobiography	Freedman, Russell
Lion, the Witch and the Wardrobe, The	Lewis, C. S.
M. C. Higgins the Great	Hamilton, Virginia
Maniac Magee	Spinelli, Jerry
Matchlock Gun, The	Edmonds, Walter
Miracles on Maple Hill	Sorensen, Virginia
Miss Hickory	Bailey, Carolyn
Missing May	Rylant, Cynthia
Misty of Chincoteague	Henry, Marguerite
Mr. Popper's Penguins	Atwater, Richard
Mrs. Frisby and the Rats of NIMH	O'Brien, Robert
My Side of the Mountain	George, Jean
Number the Stars	Lowry, Lois
Old Yeller	Gipson, Fred
On My Honor	Bauer, Marion Dane
Philip Hall Likes Me I Reckon, Maybe	Greene, Bette

Title	Author
Ramona and Her Father	Cleary, Beverly
Ramona Quimby, Age 8	Cleary, Beverly
Rascal	North, Sterling
Rifles for Watie	Keith, Harold
Roll of Thunder, Hear My Cry	Taylor, Mildred
Sarah Plain and Tall	MacLachlan, Patricia
Secret of the Andes	Clark, Ann Nolan
Shiloh	Naylor, Phyllis
Sign of the Beaver, The	Speare, Elizabeth
Slave Dancer, The	Fox, Paula
Smoky the Cow Horse	James, Will
Sounder	Armstrong, William
Strawberry Girl	Lenski, Lois
Summer of the Swans	Byars, Betsy
Thimble Summer	Enright, Elizabeth
True Confessions of Charlotte Doyle, The	Avi
Twenty-One Balloons, The	Dubois, William
Up a Road Slowly	Hunt, Irene
Voyages of Dr. Doolittle, The	Lofting, Hugh
Waterless Mountain	Armer, Laura
Westing Game, The	Raskin, Ellen
Wheel on the School, The	DeJong, Meindert
Whipping Boy, The	Fleischman, Sid
White Stag, The	Seredy, Kate
Winter Room, The	Paulson, Gary
Witch of Blackbird Pond, The	Speare, Elizabeth
Wright Brothers: How They Invented the Airplane, The	Freedman, Russell
Wrinkle in Time, A	L'Engle, Madeline
Young Mac of Fort Vancouver	Carr, Mary Jane

Regional Award
PACIFIC NORTHWEST LIBRARY ASSOCIATION
YOUNG READER'S CHOICE BOOKS

Title	Author
Black Stallion, The	Farley, Walter
Bunnicula	Howe, Deborah
By the Shores of Silver Lake	Wilder, Laura Ingalls
Chitty Chitty Bang Bang	Fleming, Ian
Cowboy Boots	Garst, Shannon
Danger in Quicksand Swamp	Wallace, Bill
Danny Dunn and the Homework Machine	Williams, Jay
Dollhouse Murders, The	Wright, Betty Ren
Golden Mare, The	Corbin, William
Homer Price	McCloskey, Robert
Incredible Journey, The	Burnford, Sheila
Indian in the Cupboard, The	Banks, Lynn Reid
John F. Kennedy and P.T. 109	Tregaskis, Richard
King of the Wind	Henry, Marguerite
Lassie Come Home	Knight, Eric
Maniac Magee	Spinelli, Jerry
Miss Pickerell Goes to Mars	MacGregor, Ellen
Mouse and the Motorcycle, The	Cleary, Beverly
Mr. Popper's Penguins	Atwater, Richard
Mrs. Frisby and the Rats of NIMH	O'Brien, Robert
Old Yeller	Gipson, Fred
Paul Bunyan Swings His Axe	McCormick, Dell
Rascal	North, Sterling
Roll of Thunder, Hear My Cry	Taylor, Mildred
Sixth Grade Can Really Kill You	De Clements, Barthe
Smoke	Corbin, William
Snow Treasure	McSwigan, Marie
Superfudge	Blume, Judy
Tales of a Fourth Grade Nothing	Blume, Judy

Title	Author
Ten Kids, No Pets	Martin, Ann
There's a Boy in the Girl's Bathroom	Sachar, Louis
Thirteen Ways to Sink a Sub	Gilson, Jamie
Wait Till Helen Comes	Hahn, Mary Downing
War with Grandpa, The	Smith, Robert Kimmell

Bibliography

Ammon, Bette and Gale W. Sherman. *Handbook for the 1992 YRCA Nominees.* Pocatello, Idaho: Beyond Basals, 1991. (Annual editions from 1988 to date.)

Alaska Association of School Librarians. *Battle of the Books Handbook.* Pacific Northwest Library Association Conference, 1985, revised 1990-91.

"Battle of the Books," *Sourdough,* July 1982, pp. 3, 22.

"The 'Battles' Continue," *School Librarian's Workshop,* November 1986, p. 8.

Children's Catalog. New York: Wilson, various editions.

The Elementary School Library Collection: A Guide to Books and Other Media. Newark, N. J.: Bro-Dart Foundation, various editions.

Goodman, Roz. "Battle of the Books, Parts I and II," *School Librarian's Workshop,* October 1985, pp. 7-8 and November 1985, pp. 4-5.

"Greater Dimensions for the Battle of the Books," *School Librarian's Workshop,* September 1988, pp. 1-3.

Greeson, Janet and Karen Taha. *Name That Book.* Metuchen, N. J.: Scarecrow, 1986.

Harshaw, Ruth and Dilla MacBean. *What Book Is That? Fun with Books at Home, at School.* New York: Macmillan, 1948.

Harshaw, Ruth and Hope Harshaw Evans. *In What Book?* New York: Macmillan, 1970.

Huck, Charlotte S., Susan Hepter, and Janet Hickman. *Children's Literature in the Elementary School,* 4th ed. New York: Holt, 1987.

Kelly, Joanne. *The Battle of Books: K-8.* Littleton, Colorado: Teacher Ideas Press, Libraries Unlimited, 1990.

———. "The 'Battle of the Books'—the Urbana Way," *School Librarian's Workshop,* April 1986, pp. 3-5.

————. "'Battle of Books' Urbana Style," *School Library Journal,* October 1982, pp. 105-8.

Kerby, Mona. "Battle of the Books," *School Library Journal,* January 1988, p. 41.

Kimmel, Margaret Mary and Elizabeth Segel. *For Reading Out Loud: A Guide to Sharing Books with Children.* New York: Delacorte, 1983.

"More 'Battle' Items," *School Librarian's Workshop,* October 1989, p. 12.

"More Notes on the 'Battle' Front," *School Librarian's Workshop,* p. 5.

"Presenting Battle of Books." District 62, Des Plaines, Illinois [1980].

"Questioning Books," *School Librarian's Workshop,* April 1988, p. 9.

Trelease, Jim. *The Readaloud Handbook.* New York: Penguin, 1985.

Trotier, Rosemary. "Follow This Game Plan," *School Library Journal,* February 1989, p. 34.

Sybilla Cook, the 1984 Oregon Elementary Library Media Teacher, is a school library consultant for several school districts in Oregon and an adjunct instructor for Western Oregon State College. She did her undergraduate work in education at Smith College and Northwestern University, and received an MALS from Rosary College (Ill.), and an MA in curriculum and instruction from the University of Oregon. She is the author of *Instructional Design for Libraries* (Garland, 1986) and *The Dewey Flipper, The Reference Flipper,* and *Referingo.* She has served on various committees for AASL as well as library associations in Illinois and Oregon.

Cheryl Page is the District Library Media Coordinator for the Roseburg (Ore.) School District. She received her educational media degree from the University of Oregon and her MS in educational communications and technology from Western Oregon State College. She is actively involved in the Oregon Educational Media Association and recently authored a document titled "Implementing the Oregon Educational Act for the 21st Century through School Library Media Programs."

Many of you who read this book are already using different types of book contests with your students. You probably have developed your own methods and procedures for managing these programs. We would appreciate hearing about all these different variations on *Books, Battles, and Bees.*

If you are willing to write and share your ideas, we will include them in any later editions of the book. Please send your ideas to:

Books, Battles, and Bees
ALA Books
50 East Huron Street
Chicago, Illinois 60611-2729